Praise for the Electronic Federal Resume Guidebook

When it comes to getting a federal job, few people know more than Kathryn Kraemer Troutman. She's been helping people outside come into government, and helping feds get promotions (or move to other agencies) for a long time. Nowadays, Troutman says the last thing anybody wants to do is walk into a federal agency with the equivalent of the old Standard Form 171. Do it, she says, and you will be ready to retire by the time you get a job.

Many agencies, including Defense, want all hiring and promotions done on an automated basis. To help 21st century DoD job hunters, Troutman has written the new "Electronic Federal Resume Guidebook and CD-ROM."

Mike Causey, www.planetgov.com, former Federal Diary Columnist, Washington Post

We would also like to thank Kathryn Kraemer Troutman, author of The Federal Resume Guidebook and Reinvention Federal Resumes for her valuable insight into preparing resumes. "According to Kathryn Troutman in Reinvention Federal Resumes, "A resume is a marketing tool. It is the very first vehicle that you have to present yourself to an anonymous person — very often to a review panel convened by a personnel specialist — and to get acquainted. An exceptional resume can move you from the "qualified" to the "best qualified" candidate category. It makes the difference between getting an interview and getting a letter that ends 'We regret to inform you ...'"

Headquarters United States Air Force, Civilian Employment and Information Handbook, May 2000

Kathy Troutman is the master of the Federal résumé! Her insight, her skill, and her years of experience are an unparalleled resource for the Federal job hunter. Follow her advice and you'll have the competitive edge in today's challenging environment!

Michael S. Dobson, author of Managing UP!, Enlightened Office Politics, and other career resources

The ELECTRONIC
Federal Resume Guidebook & CD-ROM

Kathryn Kraemer Troutman

Contributing authors
Brian Friel, Christopher Juge, Mark Reichenbacher

The Resume Place Press
Baltimore, MD

The ELECTRONIC Federal Resume Guidebook

Copyright 2001 • 116713893 by Kathryn Kraemer Troutman

ISBN 0-9647025-2-5

Published by The Resume Place Press
89 Mellor Avenue
Baltimore, MD 21228
Phone: 888-480-8265
Fax: 410-744-0112
e-mail: books@resume-place.com
Internet: www.resume-place.com

Other books by Kathryn Kraemer Troutman:

Federal Resume Guidebook & PC Disk, 1st and 2nd Editions

Reinvention Federal Resumes, 1st and 2nd Editions

The 171 Reference Book (out of print)

Creating Your High School Resume

Creating Your High School Resume, Teacher's Guide

See the back of this book for Resume Place titles and ordering information. Quantity discounts are available.

Development Editor: Barbra Guerra

Interior Designer and Interior Layout: Brian Moore

Cover Designer: Brian Moore

Proofreader: Bonita Kraemer

Glossary: Mike Ottensmeyer

CD-ROM Designers: Brian Moore and Margaret Tufty

Keywords (CD-ROM): Bonita Kraemer, Kim Hall, Margaret Tufty

CD-ROM and Appendix Resumix Resume Designs: Mark Reichenbacher

CD-ROM Private Industry Resume Designs: Bonny Kraemer Day

Printed in the United States of America by UtiliMedia • www.utilimedia.com

We have been careful to provide accurate information throughout this book, but it is possible that errors and omissions have been introduced. Web site addresses and Job Kit instructions may be updated and revised at any time. The names, social security numbers, and other information in the resumes and chapter examples are fictitious.

Trademarks: Resumix is a registered trademark of HotJobs.com, Ltd. All brand names used in this book are registered trademarks of their respective owners.

Preface

Electronic Resume Writing for DOD Civilians

I started writing this book on February 6, 2000, the day I trained about 40 human resources staff and other managers at the Naval Air Station in Pensacola, Florida. The Navy Southeast Region was going to "stand-up" the Resumix system in March with all vacancy announcements requiring a resume. More than 4,000 employees who might be applying for jobs needed to write a Resumix resume in order to be considered for these jobs! Naturally, there were many questions about how to write this resume, how to submit the resume, and how applicants were going to be selected.

I knew right then that employees needed a book about how to write the new electronic resume and to help them understand all of the new application processes. Was I ever right!

In 1995, I wrote the *Federal Resume Guidebook* when the Office of Personnel Management decided it was time to accept resumes in government. That book has helped thousands of people write their resumes. The Federal resume is accepted throughout government now, but it's been almost six years. Here's a sample of the kind of e-mails I get now from people who read my first book:

Dear Kathryn:

I purchased your Federal Resume Guidebook in October and applied for a new position with an agency that I have worked with for 14 years. I contacted you and asked some questions and you were very helpful.

Twenty-five applied for the same position. Nine candidates were qualified. Four received an interview and one was selected. You guessed it: I landed the job. I guess the other 24 didn't read your book. :-)

Thanks so much. I just received the best Christmas gift of them all. I will continue to tell everyone about your book.

Happy Holidays, December 2000

I hope this new ELECTRONIC, DOD-edition, will be as successful in helping the 600,000+ civilians get selected and promoted.

The *ELECTRONIC Federal Resume Guidebook & CD-ROM* was not an easy book to write. If the book were about resume writing only, it wouldn't be so difficult. But when you add the Federal human resources policies and procedures to the instruction manual, it gets more difficult.

I thought it would be printed by the end of September 2000, but I was invited to train for Navy and Marines so often that I lacked the time to finish the book. I did learn a lot about what you needed to know about writing a clear, focused, active, and keyword-packed resume: everything! Some civilians haven't updated their SF-171s in 2 to 15 years! That's because the SF-171 was so difficult to update! This book is based on the questions asked in my workshops, examples given, and the exercises that I have developed and used in more than 150 workshops.

And then to make writing the book more difficult, during the Summer and Fall, many of the Navy regions changed their vacancy announcement instructions to add a self-nomination link called "Application Express," the Resume Builder was redesigned, and the Additional Data Sheet is being simplified. In December, the Air Force changed the way they will be using Resumix and it may change again. I had to rewrite the "Job Kits Made Easier" chapter three times. So beware: this book and especially the Job Kits, are a work in progress. Things are changing all the time. You will have to read the directions on vacancy announcements, even with this book in hand. The resume-writing chapters are actually pretty stable. Resume writing really doesn't change, but the application processes might.

I have done my best to explain each agency's application and review process. I want this new system to work for you, the applicant, Human Resources, and the selecting officials. I believe the electronic system is here to stay and that it will be better in the long run. You need the sample resumes on the CD-ROM and the "Job Kits Made Easier." If you can write a good resume and understand the application process, you can master this new application process. This is the way people are being recruited and selected in private industry all over the world, so you might as well start writing your resume.

I know you can write a great resume detailing your career by following the chapters and samples included in this book. Believe in yourself and you will be selected.

Kathryn Kraemer Troutman
Author, President, The Resume Place, Inc. www.resume-place.com

Comments by an Electronic Human Resources Director

The transition from compiling the old SF-171 applications to the preparation and submission of electronic resumes for processing by automated staffing systems has been a traumatic event for thousands of Federal employees. Some have leaped into this new era quite successfully. Most employees, however, are still saddled with the SF-171 mentality of the past, and they have failed to grasp the essential requirements of resume preparation. Federal human resource offices bear some of the responsibility for current employee confusion because they have focused almost entirely on resume format and have neglected to teach applicants how to prepare *resume content*.

Fortunately, Kathryn Troutman has come to the rescue just in the nick of time. She has developed a book that "goes back to basics" and explains how to prepare the content of a resume. Sure, she addresses standard issues relative to format, but she concentrates on telling readers how to decide what to include in a resume, how to describe knowledge, skills, and abilities with the written word, and how to use electronic resumes in the most advantageous manner. The availability of this information is important. It will empower applicants for the first time and enable them to finally tackle this electronic resume "project" with a positive attitude and some degree of hope.

The other, very significant feature of this book — one which commends it to Federal job seekers — is that it has been prepared specifically to address the use of electronic resumes in the Federal sector. There are a glut of pamphlets and books on the market that purport to tell readers everything they need to know about electronic resume preparation, but they all deal with general characteristics without the benefit of any particular context and have been written by authors who have little or no actual "hands-on" familiarity with the practical workings of electronic resume-processing systems as they function in government.

Not so with Kathryn. As a former member of the *govexec.com* magazine staff, she writes about Federal human resource issues every week in her column, Career Corner (now located at www.resume-place.com). As a successful electronic resume-writing trainer for the Navy, Air Force, and Army, Kathryn teaches employees how to convert SF-171 content to the new resume format. She has made a profession of studying the conversion to electronic resumes in the Federal human resource world through her global resume-writing and Federal job-consulting business.

Finally, Kathryn's first book, the *Federal Resume Guidebook* has set the standard for Federal resume writing in government. The new "electronic" version is the same easy-to-read-and-understand writing style. Kathryn has studied virtually every electronic staffing program in Government, put almost all related Web sites under a microscope, analyzed every facet of resume use, and has saved readers the time and effort involved in sifting through this mass of information to find out *what works* in the Federal arena.

Does this Federal-only research and focus really make a difference? You bet it does! The processes, the requirements, the constraints — the MENTALITY — used to identify candidates and fill Federal positions are as different as night and day from those employed by the private sector. Federal personnelists ask the off-the-shelf software used in most electronic staffing programs to perform functions never envisioned by its designers. Crediting plans are generally structured to require much more detailed information than that sought by more flexible private sector headhunters. As a result, applicants for Federal positions are under greater duress to include much more meat in the same limited resume space than applicants applying for private sector positions. Of course, this "meat" (substance) must also be recognizable and creditable as the software does its job.

Intimidating? Yes. Impossible? Not at all, because Ms. Troutman has removed the confusion, discarded the bells and whistles, and has reduced the resume preparation process to its bottom line and most cogent elements. The examples provided (drawn from real, functioning electronic staffing programs) and the analysis furnished clarify and reinforce the most important steps and characteristics relevant to good electronic resume preparation.

Invest the time; read this book carefully; learn from it; apply its teachings faithfully; and your potential for success in the Federal job market will increase dramatically. The best part is that Kathryn has provided the expertise and done the really difficult work for you — the "how to" part. Your only task is to write the resume and reap the rewards!

John C. Wines
Federal Human Resource Manager

Electronic Federal Resume Writing reviewed by Rebecca A. Smith, Author, Electronic Resumes and Online Networking

The process of applying for any Federal agency job has a reputation for being time consuming, complex, and complicated. You have to re-read the instructions every time you apply for a different Federal position announcement.

Combine that with database technology and your course of action can become downright overwhelming.

At last, there is an understandable solution that brings clarity to this daunting process: Kathryn Troutman's *Electronic Federal Resume Guidebook*.

Kathy starts off presenting a big picture overview of how the Resumix resume database works. Resumix is the database used by Department of Defense agencies to digitally store and retrieve resumes. The reader then learns how the Department of Defense uses Resumix as its standard for capturing resume data on employees as well as new applicants.

One of the most innovative concepts in this highly readable book is the Job Kits Made Easier for four major agencies. She analyzed each job kit for similarities and presented a simplified, paper version to help you apply correctly for jobs in each of the services. Kathy gives you the inside scoop on how the software extracts skills from your "Skills Bucket," a nice metaphor to clarify a technically complex process.

By combining this information with the use of the Resume Builders, you will no longer have to second-guess if you are writing your Electronic Federal Resume and applying for a job correctly.

Learn from Kathy how to take advantage of position announcements to find those elusive keywords and phrases that are essential to your success in the Federal job market.

Kathy is a pioneer in the design and distribution of the Federal Resume. Now it is time to take your Federal Resume to the next level with her *ELECTRONIC Federal Resume Guidebook*.

I've known Kathy for several years now, and we have yet to meet face-to-face. Yet in that time, Kathy and I have watched each other grow intellectually and as businesswomen. We've written books, become subject matter experts, speakers and trainers, while living on opposite sides of the United States. This is the tremendous power of electronic communication. Now you can use this power to achieve more in less time and get on the electronic Federal Resume bandwagon.

Rebecca Smith
Author and Online Educator
Electronic Resumes and Online Networking
Career Press, Second Edition
Fremont, California

Resume Writing Tips for Civilians Affected by Commercial Activities Studies, Brian Friel, Senior Editor, www.govexec.com

If you're a civilian employee of the Defense Department or one of the military services, we don't have to tell you this is a time of great upheaval for the civil servants who support our nation's defense.

From the late 1980s to the late 1990s, downsizing, base closures, the end of the Cold War, changing military strategies, and information technology advances combined to reduce the civilian workforce from 1.1 million employees in 1987 to 700,000 employees in 1999.

Pentagon officials say about 100,000 additional positions will be eliminated by 2005. To accomplish that goal, the Defense Department is putting 200,000 jobs up for auction to the lowest bidder. As Defense Department employees defend their jobs, private-sector contractors are placing bids for the work. The idea is that competition will spur Federal workers to become more efficient.

Whether you agree with the Pentagon's competition plans, the trend in the defense establishment is toward using practices common in private companies to improve operations. In addition to the public-private competitions for jobs, the Defense Department is starting to use recruiting and hiring techniques that are standard practice in the private sector.

One of those techniques is the electronic resume.

On the surface, electronic resumes are not much different from paper resumes. Both include basic information about job applicants: name, contract information, employment history, educational background, descriptions of skills, and experiences.

But behind the scenes, electronic resumes are much different. Paper resumes are submitted for specific job vacancies, vetted by human resources staff and passed on to hiring managers. That system works fine for small organizations and for positions with few applicants.

But for large corporations and positions with thousands of applicants, a paper-based system becomes a nightmare to manage. In the late 1980s and early 1990s, several entrepreneurs saw a market opportunity and began developing computer systems to manage job applications. Large corporations were their first clients. Using the new systems, large corporations hired clerks to physically scan thousands of resumes into the electronic systems. Companies soon had databases with tens of thousands of resumes. If a job vacancy came up, managers would simply plug some key skill requirements into the resume systems, and a list of potential job applicants would appear.

The Defense Department began eyeing these systems in the early 1990s, and in 1995 began the process of getting those systems up and running across its vast organization. Through pilot phases and several fits and starts, those systems are now generally in place. The Defense Finance Accounting Service-Kansas City and Navy are the farthest along the path to successfully utilize their electronic resume systems. The Air Force, Army, and other Defense agencies are a bit farther behind.

Employees of most Defense Department units that are using electronic resume systems are required to update their resumes. In some cases, outside job applicants are also required to submit resumes that can be put in the electronic systems.

The systems, if all goes according to officials' plans, will have a profound effect on how civilian job vacancies are filled in the Defense Department. Until now, DOD has operated much like a small organization with few job applicants, using a paper-based system. That process was good for the applicant, because it meant each applicant got a personal review of his or her application. In addition, the applicant was guaranteed the opportunity to be considered for the specific positions he or she was interested in.

But from hiring officials' perspective, that paper-based system meant a long, tedious process before being able to fill positions. Under the electronic resume system, applicants will submit their resumes for specific positions and they will use a new process, "self-nomination," to apply for additional jobs. Hiring officials will then search the resume databases for anyone who might have the mix of qualifications they're looking for.

Employees facing the specter of outsourcing have the incentive of getting their resumes into the electronic system so that they can be considered for more stable positions than the ones they hold, which could disappear through the A-76 process. Whether their current positions are eliminated or not, it makes career sense to get their resumes into consideration for other positions throughout the Defense Department.

Taking the time to prepare their resumes for the internal Defense Department databases holds another career benefit. In the event a contractor position becomes available to them, civilian employees can use their new resumes to apply to private firms — firms that would be loath to pore through a voluminous SF-171.

Let's not sugarcoat this. Both the outsourcing/A-76 trend and the shift to electronic resume systems are less than ideal developments for career civil servants. But they are the reality of the times, and both underscore the importance of this book. You could let the trends sweep you along, or you could be prepared for whatever fate these developments deal you.

It is time for you to prepare an electronic resume.

BrianFriel,
Senior Editor

www.govexec.com

Organization of the Book

Civilian Activities Studies and Your Resume
Brian Friel, senior editor of www.govexec.com, writes about his knowledge of commercial activities in civilian Department of Defense agencies. He correlates these studies to the importance of individual resume writing. Read this to get inspired to write this resume right away!

How Electronic Resume Technology Works
Matching jobs to people. An introduction to the DOD electronic resume systems.

Skills Extraction and Your "Skills Bucket"
The software extracts skills from your resume. Your resume is turned into a "skills bucket" in the system. Learn how important the right skills are for the recruitment searches.

Job Kits Made Easier
Each human resources office has written slightly different instructions for writing and submitting your resume. This is a review and orientation of the Job Kits. After you read about the basics, it will be less intimidating. Most of the official civilian Job Kits are on the CD-ROM.

What Happens to Your Resume
This chapter answers all of your questions about how the new system works — step-by-step. It covers the resume submission, the hiring manager's request to hire, the selection and job offer process.

Getting Qualified
Two HR managers explain how they find the "cream of the crop." John Wines, Director, Kansas City Customer Support Unit for the Defense Finance and Accounting Service, and Stephen Janik, Army Civilian Personnel Advisory Center (CPAC), describe their different processes for qualifying, rating and ranking candidates for the hiring manager's consideration.

Research the Announcements
Learn how to analyze announcements in an "analytical method" to find the skills and specialized language to describe your knowledge, skills and abilities. Use these words in your resume to improve your searchability and success.

One Resume Fits All
Learn how to write one resume that covers multiple job interests. It's easier than ever to write one thorough resume for the database.

Work Experience
90% of the resumes and the searchable information is found in the Work Experience section. Four sections are devoted to help you write a clear, understandable, and impressive explanation of your duties and accomplishments at work.

Getting Started
We show a case study of a Carpenter/Electronics Technician who is seeking a job with a civilian DOD agency. We take him through the research process with three job databases (Army, Air Force, and Navy). We select the appropriate job titles, analyze announcements for skills, decide what to keep in his resume, organize his jobs, integrate skills from the announcements, and write his electronic resume.

Resume Writing Lessons

Hats, Nouns, and Skills
How many hats do you wear at work? What roles do you play in your job? Using nouns and verbs, create an outline of your job based on your official and unofficial job titles. This outline will be the basis of your new description of your duties.

Fill in Your Outline
Write clear, active voice descriptions following the outline you created above. If you are a manager, write about your responsibilities as a Supervisor and Team Leader, Contract Manager, Customer Liaison, Budget Manager, and Agency Representative. If you are a secretary, write about your responsibilities as an Office Coordinator or Administrator, Computer Operator, Scheduler, Meeting Coordinator, Travel Planner, and Public Relations and Client Point of Contact.

What Have You Accomplished Lately?
The Job Kits ask for "Duties and Accomplishments." Federal employees from resume-writing workshops share their accomplishments. Get inspired to write about your projects and accomplishments. Remember the old saying, "It ain't braggin' if you done it!"

Don't Forget Your KSAs
You have certain knowledge, skills and abilities in order to perform your job. Even though you do not have to write separate KSAs any longer (wonderful

new feature of the automated system), you still need to include your knowledge, skills and abilities in your work experience write-up.

Putting It All Together
The Work Experience section of your resume is the most important section of the resume. Tips and Frequently Asked Questions for writing the Work Experience section of your resume are included.

Resume Builders and Other Information
Examples and instructions for writing the rest of your resume: personal information, education, training, other qualifications, and soft skills.

Resume Writing and Editing Tips

Plain Language Resumes
Learn how to turn your bureaucratic writing style into an easy-to-read and interesting document. There are many examples of bureaucratic language to edit out of your resume.

Dos and Don'ts
A checklist to remind you that you're not writing a regular Federal resume or a private industry resume.

Appendix

Two samples of the new electronic resume.

Job Kits and Web site addresses for finding vacancy announcements, instructions, and Resume Builders on agency human resources Web sites.

The CD-ROM — Resources, Research, and Resumes

Job Kits
We have researched the latest available official job kits from Navy, Air Force and Army Web sites. You will become familiar with the official instructions. As time goes by the Job Kits may change, so visit the Web sites listed to make sure the most recent instructions are available. The Air Force Web site and instructions will be changing in the near future.

Keywords and KSAs
120 Federal occupations are analyzed here for keywords. We searched vacancy announcements and analyzed duties and responsibilities for the skills that could be included in your resume. Our research and skills are just the beginning for your research. We took only one vacancy announcement for each occupation and analyzed the content. We do not have all available skills for each series. Use these keywords as examples and research your own list for your resume.

Private Industry Resumes
Five of the electronic Federal resumes are re-designed for private industry. These resumes could be used for private industry or can be sent to government contractors who are competing for Federal jobs.

Electronic Resume Samples
The samples are available for you to study the content, writing style, and format. They are also excellent to use as templates. You simply save one of the files and replace text throughout the resume to create your own resume. This can save hours of time when writing your resume.

Acknowledgments

This book has been created out of my hundreds of training classes with the Navy, Marine, and Air Force civilian employees. First, I'd like to thank Victoria Knight and the workshop participants from Center for Naval Education and Training, Pensacola, Florida. Hundreds of CNET employees brought their Merit Promotion forms and evaluations to class and began writing their Resumix resumes during the workshop. They wrote a list of duties and accomplishments and completed an amazing amount of their electronic resumes during that one day.

I'd also like to thank Minnie Polite, Training Coordinator, and the workshop participants from USMC Materiel Command, Albany, Georgia, who shared outstanding accomplishments which are written in the "What have you accomplished?" section.

From the Navy, I'd like to thank Dale Farley, Resumix Team Leader, NAS Pensacola, FL who sponsored my first Resumix Navy training program. Resumix Team Leaders and Human Resources managers who communicated with me throughout the research of the book included: Paula Hodge, former Resumix Team Leader, Navy SE HROC; Lisa Becker, Navy Resumix Team; Thomas Martinez, Navy NCR HROC; and Debbie Lee, Navy Resumix Project Manager, Silverdale, Washington. Debbie was also supportive in 1995 when I wrote the *Federal Resume Guidebook*.

From the Air Force, I'd like to thank Tom Carroll, Standard Automated Inventory and Referral System (STAIRS) Program Manager, HQ AF/PMO-PC; Felipe Jimenez, HQ AF/DPFAZ; and James C. McDaniel III, PALACE Acquire Administrator, Communications & Information Career Program for their information on The Air Force Personnel Center system.

From the Army, I'd like to thank Steve Janik and Joe Barnes for their review and contributions to the Army Job Kit Made Easier and "Getting Qualified" chapter.

From DFAS-Kansas City, John Wines, Personnel Coordinator wrote many e-mails explaining their Delegated Examining Unit processes so that this book could be clear to resume writers. He also wrote the preface and contributed to the "Getting Qualified" chapter.

HotJobs.com Ltd./Resumix™ Federal Manager, Mike Jurkowski was informative and helpful through the technical questions; and Larry Grein, Director,

Resumix University, produced Skills Buckets for this book and my training classes.

Brian Friel, my first Career Corner editor at www.govexec.com and supporter through the conceptualizing of this book contributed the A-76 article. He also contributed to Chapter 1, "How Electronic Resume Technology Works" and Chapter 10, "Dos and Dont's."

Chris Juge, Resume Place SES Writer/Editor, contributed the "Plain Language" chapter for the book. He took four versions of "English Lessons" that I created and compiled them into 10 Writing Principles that I will be using in my resume-writing classes for years to come.

Bryan Hochstein, President of QuickHire, was informative and supportive in communicating their new automated system that is being used by USGS, Energy and other non-DOD agencies.

Resume sample contributors were: Burdettea Andrews, Lyn East, Deborah Viviani, Vickie Quisenberry, James Charles Stubbs, Audrea M. Nelson, Deborah Gerchow, Jene Thompson, Gilbert U. Hernandez, Alan Cross, Dennis Chiu, David Garcia, Ruth Riggins, Esmeralda Gutierrez, and Emily Harman.

My Resume Place Resume Writing and Design Team:

Bonny Day, my sister and Business Manager designed the private industry resumes; Bonita Kraemer, my mother and a former English teacher, proofread the book several times; Mark Reichenbacher edited and formatted the Resumix resume samples; Margaret Tufty who worked as my assistant on the CD-ROM through several versions; Kim Hall researched and compiled the Official Job Kits; and Lori Troutman, my 18-year-old daughter, helped me get over writer's block when I was writing the "Job Kits Made Easier" chapters.

Table of Contents

Part I – Job Kits and Instructions

PART II – New Automated Human Resources Methods

PART III – Research and Career Decision-Making

PART IV – Writing Your Resume

PART V – Editing and Formatting Tips

On the CD-ROM

Official Job Kits and Instructions, Resume Builders, Additional Data Sheets for Air Force, Army, Navy, Marines, and other DOD and Federal HR offices

Keywords and KSAs by "artificial intelligence"

Private Industry Sample Resumes

Resume Builder Log Sheet

Book Index – Available to help you find specific information in the book about resume writing and electronic job postings.

18 Electronic Resume Samples, Word Templates, and Samples for Writing Style and Information.

ADMINISTRATIVE OFFICER, GS-341-12

Program Operations Oversight

Supervisory Military Manpower Analyst, GS-205-11

Naval Air Station, Lemoore, CA

COMPUTER SPECIALIST, GS-334-13

Life Cycle Manager, Test Facility

Team Leader for Strategic Planning and Web Support

Defense Information Systems Agency, DISA, Slidell, LA

DIVISION SECRETARY, OFFICE AUTOMATION, GS-318-4

Administrative Assistant

Program Assistant

Management Assistant

Personnel Clerk/Personnel Assistant

Naval Oceanography Office, NAVOCEANO, N23,
Customer Service Division, Warfighting Support Center, Stennis Space Center, MS

EDUCATION SERVICES GUIDANCE COUNSELOR, GS-1740-9

Family Advocacy Program Instructor, Trainer

Counselor

Veterans Program Assistant

Social Worker

Department of the Army, Educational Services Division, Fort Bliss, El Paso, TX

ELECTRICAL ENGINEER, GS-850-11

Computer Specialist, GS-334-11/12

Computer System Programmer, GS-334-11

Nuclear Engineer, GS-840-12

Marine Corps Base Hawaii at Kaneohe, Hawaii

EQUIPMENT SPECIALIST TRAINEE, GS-1670-05

Electronic Integrated Systems Mechanic, WG-2610-12

Norfolk Naval Shipyard, Aircraft Maintenance Division, Avionics Maintenance
Squadron, Electrical Systems Branch, Norfolk, VA

INSTRUCTIONAL SYSTEM SPECIALIST, GS-1750-12

Installation Commander

Naval Oceanographic Office, Stennis Space Center, MS

LOCKSMITH, ELECTRONICS, WG

Maintenance Structural Trade Chief II, Carpentry Shop

University of Maryland, College Park (Veteran)

LOGISTICS SPECIALIST, GS-034-5

INVENTORY MANAGEMENT SPECIALIST, GS-2010-7

Albertsons.com, Bellevue, WA

MANAGEMENT ANALYST, GS-343-12

Program Manager / Project Analyst

Computer Specialist (Equipment Analyst), GS-334-12

Naval Education and Training Professional Development Technology Center

(NETPDTC), Pensacola, FL

MANAGEMENT/PROGRAM ANALYST, GS-343-12

Manpower Resource Planner

Command Representative

McGuire Air Force Base, AFB, Bordentown, NJ

REALTY SPECIALIST, GS-1170-7

Loan Processing Assistant, GS-1101-6

Realty Assistant, GS-303-5

U. S. Army Corps of Engineers, Sacramento, CA

SECRETARY, GS-318-5

Office Assistant

Administrative Assistant

Naval Education and Training Professional Development Technology Center,

NETPDTC, Corpus Christi, TX

SENIOR SCIENTIST, GS-XXX-14

Program Manager, GS-301

Oceanographer

Department of the Navy for major military modeling and simulation.

Office of the Secretary of Defense, Pentagon, Arlington, VA.

SHORE SITE INSTALLATION MANAGER/EQUIPMENT SPECIALIST, GS-1670-12

Contracts Administrator

Project Leader

Field Engineer

Naval Surface Warfare Center, Port Hueneme Division, Battle Force Tactical Training (BTT), Port Hueneme, CA

SUPERVISORY CONTRACT SPECIALIST, GS-1102-14

Contract Specialist

Contracting Officer

Naval Air Warfare Center, NAVAIR, Patuxent River, MD

SYSTEMS ACCOUNTANT, GS-510-12

Program Analyst, GS-343-12

Management Analyst, GS-343-12

Budget Analyst, GS-560-12

Defense Finance and Accounting Service, Headquarters, Arlington, VA

WRITER/EDITOR, GS-1082

Trainer, GS-1712

Employee Development Specialist, GS-235

Public Affairs Officer, GS-1035

The Resume Place, Inc., Baltimore, MD.

*This book is dedicated to my children
Lori, Emily, and Chris, and my sister Bonny.*

*It is also dedicated to the thousands of civilians who
need to write a great resume so they can get promoted
and challenged in new jobs!*

Part 1
Job Kits and Instructions

Chapter 1
How Electronic Resume Technology Works

Chapter 2
Skills Extraction and Your "Skills Bucket"

Chapter 3
Job Kits Made Easier
   Air Force
   Army
   Defense Finance and Accounting Service - Kansas City
   Navy / Marines

Chapter 1

How Electronic Resume Technology Works

Getting selected for a new job or promotion will depend on how well you understand the new electronic recruitment and selection process . . . and how well you write your resume!

Automated Human Resources History — The Electronic Resume Database

Department of Defense agencies are now mandated and equipped to use software and information technology to handle job applications. There are three events that led to the Department of Defense adopting a new method for filling position vacancies within their civil service programs.

The first event was the National Performance Review (NPR), the initiative to reinvent the Federal government and to streamline its operations and processes. One of the initiatives was the recommendation to use a resume in government instead of the long historical SF-171 in order to facilitate automation of the application process.

The second event was the DOD Program Decision Memorandum (PDM), which directed regionalization of civilian personnel operations in all branches of the armed forces to achieve efficiency. As a result of the PDM, the Modern Defense Civilian Personnel Data System was developed and Resumix was selected as the automated staffing system to be used by all DOD components and agencies. Resumix is a commercial off-the-shelf software product that uses artificial intelligence to read resumes. MDCPDS and Resumix replaced existing 171 and KSA applications and the manual Delegated Examining rating process.

The third event was Program Budget Decision 711, the directive in 1999 that cut the number of civilian personnelists in the Federal government in half. To the Air Force, this meant going from approximately 3,000 personnelists to 1,500. The reduction in personnel staff required the change to an automated staffing process — away from large paper applications.

Because of these three events, DOD agencies adopted a new process that involves the use of resumes and self-nomination. The new system is designed to provide an automated promotion and referral system. The Resumix system extracts skills and rates and ranks candidates for job selection. You no longer have to prepare lengthy applications and submit separate ones for each vacancy announcement. Once you submit a resume, you may use that single resume to compete for all vacancy announcements for which you desire placement consideration.

Once you have an understanding of the system, it will be faster and easier to apply for jobs.

How Human Resources Recruiters Search for You

The HR recruiter's search for qualified candidates is like using an Internet search engine. You've probably used search engines such as AltaVista, Yahoo!, or Ask.com. You type in a keyword or phrase, click submit, and the search engine — seconds later — returns a list of links to Web sites with that keyword or phrase on it. Each search engine site originates from a database that stores information from millions of Web pages. When you type in a keyword, the search engine looks through its database to find matching links.

Resumix and electronic resume systems use similar technology. Although they're more sophisticated than Internet search engines, the system works basically the same way:

1. A DOD agency creates a database of resumes.

2. When a job opening comes up, a manager or human resources specialist types in key required skills.

3. Resumes with matching skills are listed for the selecting manager or HR specialist.

Simply put, electronic resume systems make an attempt to match the right person with the right job.

Resumix and Other Automated Human Resources Systems

As many as 60 electronic resume systems are on the market. For example, Webhire, a company based in Lexington, Massachusetts, has a central database of about two million resumes that hundreds of private companies search through for job candidates. RezLogic of Colorado Springs, Colorado, makes an electronic resume system called RezKeeper, which is used by a number of large companies. Other non-DOD agencies are using QuickHire from Alexandria, Virginia. The U.S. Geological Survey and the Department of Interior have been successful with this system. Their Job Kits are on the CD-ROM in this book.

The Department of Defense has selected an electronic resume system from Resumix, owned by HotJobs.com, Ltd. of Sunnyvale, California., to manage the hundreds of thousands of resumes it receives from job seekers each year, as well as the resumes for the more than 600,000 civilian workers the Department, military services, and defense agencies employ.

According to Resumix, its system has built-in intelligence that "actually recognizes the contextual meaning of words within a resume by extracting relevant information with pinpoint accuracy." In other words, if a Defense Department hiring official is looking for someone with Web site management skills, Resumix would know if a person has Web site management skills, even if his or her resume lists skills in "Web development" or "managing Web-based applications" or "running Internet and intranet sites."

How the Search Process Works: Matching Skills with Position Descriptions

But let's back up a moment. Before an HR specialist begins a search of the resume database, he or she must first write a position description (known as a PD) for a job opening. Before an HR specialist could begin the search of the resume database, the supervisor writes a current position description for the position. Once the position description is written, the key skills are identified and the match begins!

Example #1: Boiler Plant Operator

The HR recruiter at the U.S. Military Academy at West Point is looking for a Boiler Plant Operator. The Boiler Plant Manager and an HR specialist have created a position description. The required skills they've compiled include the ability to make repairs to plumbing facilities, experience testing boiler plant systems for leaks and performing preventive maintenance, and experience supervising entry-level mechanics. The manager wants someone with at least two years of experience as a Boiler Plant Operator.

The HR specialist then enters the position description into the Resumix system and searches either in an occupational inventory of resumes or a self-nominated inventory of resumes. The recruiter asks the system to find resumes from candidates with matching skills and experience.

Resumix then returns a list of resumes that match. The recruiter hopes for at least 15 qualified candidates whose resumes match the search list.

An HR specialist can set a number of criteria that limit the number of candidates returned by Resumix. These criteria might include:

* **Specific skills:** For example, Watertube boilers and full steam generation support equipment, ASME certified welder, quality boiler service, supervisor, incinerator repair, preventive mainte nance plans, steam system surveys. (These keywords were found at http://www.boiler.net/operations.html. This Web site was found through searching www.altavista.com under Boiler Plant Operator.)

* **Previously held Job titles:** Boiler Plant Operator, Power Plant Operator, Mechanical Engineer, Facilities Manager, Property Manager.

* **Years of experience:** At least 2 years hands-on experience.

* **Type of degree(s):** Not mandatory, but a B.S. in Mechanical Engineering could be a search term.

* **Certification:** A certification may or may not be required, but they may search for ASME or OSHA standards.

* **GPA:** This would probably not be a search criteria.

* **Geographic location:** This is an important search element, the selecting official may wish to select a local candidate.

An HR specialist can fine-tune the request even further by specifying that a specialized skill or qualification is required or just desired. For example, experience with CB Cleaver-Brooks may be mandatory for this job.

After completing a search and coming up with a list of qualified candidates, the HR specialist forwards the list of "Certified" candidates (the Cert) and the paper resumes to the selecting official, who then selects and interviews the top candidates.

Example #2: Education Services Specialist

A Navy Education Services Supervisor seeks to hire an Education Services Specialist. The selecting official would like as many qualified internal and external applicants as possible. He requested a search on three specific skills (typically they search for 4 to 8 skills), in addition to education and years of experience. Thirty resumes came up as qualified with all three specific skills and educational qualifications in their resumes This is the information that could be in the position description and in the matching resumes:

* **Specific skills:** The following skills could be in their resume: Assessment, interview, community outreach, marketing, career services, student orientation, financial advice, curriculum design, job search strategies, advocacy, co-op educational programs, Educational Assistance Programs (EAP), military personnel records, research.

* **Job titles:** Applicant job titles could be Guidance Counselor, Career Counselor, Distance Learning Counselor, Educational Specialist, Education Technician, Placement Officer, Test Control Officer, Trainer, Financial Advisor, Tuition Assistance Advisor, Career Strategy Advisor,

* **Years of experience:** At least 4 years hands-on experience.

* **Type of degree(s):** B.S. or M.S. in Education or other major.

* **Certification:** None required

* **GPA:** This would be optional for the selecting official to require a certain GPA.

* **Geographic location:** The HR office may or may not pay for relocation. Typically they will look for people who are local to the area, but they may be flexible and consider other geographic areas.

 Tip   If your resume can match a PD, that could result in a successful candidate search!

How to Apply

The HR staff can search for resumes in three ways:

* Through the entire inventory of resumes in a specific job series

* Through self-nominated candidates

* By reading 171s, 612s, resumes, and KSAs (the old way and destined for obsolescence)

The resumes in the first category belong to candidates who have selected particular occupations. These candidates have put their resumes into the database with an "inventory building" announcement. You will learn how to submit your resume into an inventory building announcement later in book.

Job Announcement # 1 — Inventory Building Announcement

The following is an example of a Job Opportunity Announcement soliciting this type of resume.

**INVENTORY-BUILDING ANNOUNCEMENT
GENERATING AN APPLICANT POOL — CLOSES 2002**

Announcement Number: SE1740

Announcement Date: 02/14/2000

Title: EDUCATION SERVICES SPECIALIST

Pay Plan: GS/DEMO

Series: 1740

Grade: Multiple Grades

Opening Date: 02/14/2000

Closing Date: 02/14/2002

Location: Southeast Geographic Area, Various locations serviced by HRSC-SE.

How to apply: The Human Resources Service Center Southeast (HRSCSE) is soliciting resumes to fill current and/or future vacancies in this occupational series. THIS ANNOUNCEMENT WILL BE USED TO GENERATE AN APPLICANT POOL FOR POTENTIAL VACANCIES. INTERESTED APPLICANTS SHOULD APPLY NOW. NO FURTHER ANNOUNCEMENTS WILL BE ISSUED ON INDI-VIDUAL VACANCIES.

Job Announcement # 2 — Electronic Resume and Self-Nomination

Here's a second example of this type of announcement.

SPECIFIC JOB ANNOUNCEMENT OPENED 11/13/2000 AND CLOSES 11/28/20000 REQUIRING A RESUME AND SELF-NOMINATION

U.S. Army, Aberdeen, MD

HOW TO APPLY: Your Resumix resume should already be in the database; Self-Nominate for this position. If you wait to the last minute to submit your resume to the Resume Builder, it may not get to the Civilian Training Operation Center (CPOC) in time. It's best to put the resume into the database early, then look for an announcement and self-nominate.

If you are currently serviced by the Northeast Civilian Personnel Operation Center, you must have a resume on file with our office to self-nominate. Employees may submit a resume at any time; however, we cannot guaran-tee the resume will be processed by the closing date of the announcement. If you are submitting your resume in response to this announcement, please note you will also need to include your self-nomination. For assistance, you may contact your local Civilian Personnel Advisory Center.

To self-nominate, give your Name; SSN; Announcement Number; Position Title, Pay Plan, Series, Grade of the Position you are applying for; Work and/ or Home Telephone Numbers; lowest acceptable grade/salary; and typing and/or steno dictation speed words per minute (if applicable). If the position has a mandatory education requirement, please certify as to whether you meet the requirement and how. See Where to Submit Package for self-nomination address.

Job Announcement # 3 — Paper Application – 171, 612, Resume and KSAs

And yet another example.

DOD AGENCY VACANCY ANNOUNCEMENT REQUIRING SF-171, OF-612, SUPPLEMENTAL STATEMENTS.

US Army Engineering Research and Development Center, Champlain, IL

HOW TO APPLY: All applicants must complete and sign the attached Supplemental Qualification Statement (SQS). Applicants must provide two (2) sets of copies of their signed SQS and SF171, OF612, DA Form 2302, or resume and a copy of their most recent performance appraisal when applying against this announcement. Applications WILL NOT be accepted by fax or e-mail. NOTE: Do NOT use the Resume Builder button provided below to submit your resume. RESUMIX will NOT be used to fill these vacancies. ELECTRONIC APPLICATIONS CANNOT BE ACCEPTED.

Submitting Your Electronic Resume for Future Searching

When you find a vacancy announcement that matches your experience, read the directions for HOW TO APPLY. Also be sure to read WHO CAN APPLY. You never can tell who can apply for DOD jobs. It can be open to anyone, or it may be limited to the local geographic area. Submit your resume into the correct resume builder depending on the vacancy announcement. The Human Resources office will receive your resume within a short time for consideration of a particular job, or to be part of a database.

The software Resumix turns your resume into a "resume summary" (also known as your "Skills Bucket" which is covered in Chapter 2) that lists all the skills the system identified in your resume. The summary also includes information about your education, work experience, and other qualifications. You can see a sample of a "Resume Summary" or "Skills Bucket" at the end of Chapter 2.

Your resume summary will wait in the Resumix database (instead of a filing cabinet) for an HR recruiter specialist to search for someone with your particular set of skills and qualifications.

Chapter Review

Resumix is the system being used by Department of Defense agencies to manage resumes and search for qualified candidates. Understanding the new automated human resources processes and *how to apply* is more challenging than ever. Read the directions in each announcement in order to successfully apply for a job the new electronic way.

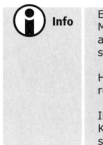 **Info**

Everything is new with human resources because of technology. Most announcements state "SF-171, OF-612 or KSAs will not be accepted!" All you have to do is write one good resume and start submitting it to the various databases.

Hiring Managers like the new automated system because of the reduced time it takes to get a list of qualified candidates.

Internal applicants are relieved they don't have to write separate KSAs any longer. But they do have to make sure their knowledge, skills, and abilities are included in the text of their resumes.

Fact Sheet
Electronic Resume and Automated Application Processes in DOD Agencies

* Resume Only — DOD agencies will not accept the SF-171 or OF-612 as a job application for most applications.

* Resume Builder — use the Resume Builder to submit your resume so you can return to update your resume anytime.

* Each DOD agency has different Resume Builders and Data bases. There isn't one database for all DOD employees or candidates. The Navy has eight databases; Army has ten databases; Air Force has one database.

* Content is most important in your Resumix resume. The HR recruiters will search for you using keywords and skills that should be included in your resume

* There are three kinds of vacancy announcements:

  1. Inventory building announcements — database collection announcements for applicants who want to be considered for future unannounced jobs.

  2. Real announcements — for specific, current job openings with closing dates requiring a self-nomination plus resume.

  3. The old way — announcements that still allow the applicant to submit a resume (can be the Resumix in the Resume Builder), OF-612, or SF-171, and separately written KSAs.

* Read the directions in the announcement and the agency's Job Kit!

* Hiring, selection, e-mails and telephone calls for qualified candidates are MUCH FASTER with the new automated system.

Chapter 2

Skills Extraction and Your "Skills Bucket" (Skills Summary)

Get to know your "skills bucket"!

When you copy and paste your resume into a Resume Builder and hit Submit, your resume goes into a database. Your resume becomes a "skills bucket." This is the term for your resume skills in Resumix. This chapter explains how the skills in your resume will be extracted into your very own skills bucket, in other words — skills summary. More than ever before, it is imperative that you write a focused, concise, and thoughtful resume that contains the right words. These words comprise your own personal skills bucket.

Which are the right words? You have to find the words that represent your knowledge, skills, and abilities for a certain occupation. Once you read this chapter, you will have a better understanding of the types of skills and words that will be searchable in the database. The CD-ROM has many examples of skills buckets and key words extracted from resumes and vacancy announcements. After you come to understand your key words and the significance of your skills bucket, you will be able to write a better resume that will result in being qualified for your desired positions. Your career depends on it.

Automated HR Jargon

We're trying to avoid "techno-speak" words and human resources jargon in this book, but this chapter will be an exception. If you're a Defense Department employee, you probably already have tons of jargon spinning through your head: MEO, PWS, A-76, micropurchases, integrated product teams, total asset visibility, and our favorite, PCS (for permanent change of station) — why can't people just say they moved?

We're going to encourage you to use fewer acronyms and jargon in your electronic resume too. The databases may not have all of your acronyms, so you should spell them out and edit them as much as you can.

Throughout this book you'll see that we have to add to the jargon whirlwind in DOD agencies because of the new electronic resume application process. You're going to be learning many new terms, such as: skills bucket, skills extraction, general and local grammar, knowledge base, artificial intelligence, and Optical Character Recognition (OCR) to describe your resume and the words in it. Here goes your first Electronic Resume Vocabulary Lesson.

Definitions

Self-Nomination and Application Express: To apply for a particular job by self-nominating, which is usually an email or form that you will find in the vacancy announcement or on the website where the announcements are posted. First you submit you resume to a database, then you self-nominate for particular jobs.

Skills Bucket: Your resume will become a skills bucket (skills summary) when it is in the Resumix system database. See a sample skills bucket in this chapter.

Skills Extraction: The automated system uses optical character recognition to recognize and extract words that are skills from your resume.

199 Skills: The Resumix system can recognize and list a total of 199 skills, which will be in your skills bucket.

General Grammar: The Resumix System has a knowledge base made up of 40,000 general grammar skills and phrases, technical terms from jobs available everywhere. The same general grammar is used for DOD employers and private industry employers.

Local Grammar: Each employer — Navy, Air Force, Marines, and Army — will add its specific local grammar to a database made up of terminology from the specific employer. You cannot depend on the local grammar to include all of your acronyms.

Artificial Intelligence: This is a combination of the skills database and the programming for recognizing and extracting skills. The Resumix system "reads" sentences in context for the right meaning of words.

The Knowledge Base: This base is made up of the general and local grammar mentioned above.

Magic Skills: "Magic skills" are specific terms that a recruiter will use to search for qualified candidates.

Paper Resume: This will be a paper printout of your resume as seen by a hiring manager — if you have the right magic skills in your resume during the search. You still have to write your resume considering human readers!

Job Kit: The Job Kit is the set of instructions written by agencies on how to apply for a job in an automated system and how to write an acceptable resume. The Official Job Kits are on the CD-ROM of this book.

Dictionary of Occupational Titles: A valuable encyclopedic source that describes most jobs in today's job market, using the specific grammar, terms, and skills language that can be used in an electronic resume.

How Does the System Create a Skills Bucket?

When your resume is submitted into a database, an automatic skills extraction process takes place. Your resume will be turned into a "skills bucket" made up of 199 verbs, nouns, skills, and interpersonal traits that have been extracted from your resume.

The HR recruiters search in the database for particular keywords that will be in your resume skills bucket.

For example, if there's a line in your resume that says you "managed and directly supervised 65 professional and administrative staff across three divisions," Resumix identifies "personnel supervision" as one of your skills. Then Resumix adds that phrase to your skills bucket. If a hiring official is looking for someone with experience supervising personnel, Resumix will list you as a candidate.

That's skills extraction in a nutshell.

Your Magic Skills

The most important skills in your bucket are the "magic skills," the four to six skills that will be used to search for qualified candidates. There might be a total of 300 to 3,000 resumes in a particular occupational series or "self-nominated" group. The recruiter will search for resumes with the same four to eight skills to find a desired 15 to 30 candidates.

We don't know what these four to eight magic skills are. That is the unknown factor of the system. The hiring managers decide which four skills are the searchable terms. If you write a good and complete resume that describes your knowledge, skills, abilities, and accomplishments, your resume will include these skills. It is proven that a well-written resume will be successful with the skills extraction system. Applicants receive e-mails every day identifying successful matches on keywords and skills.

Skills Extraction Demonstration

Here's an excerpt from a computer specialist's electronic resume:

> Project leader or lead analyst/software engineer in directing the efforts of journeyman software engineers assigned to projects. Develop computer applications in support of management systems, policies, and regulatory requirements. Perform fact finding and research necessary to determine the nature and scope of a new requirement or change to be developed, the amount and type of source data to be utilized and the end products to be produced for client/server applications developed with Oracle Developer 2000 in a Oracle database environment. Prepare software engineering specifications, hierarchical structure interfaces, data views, major processes, controls and system test plans.

Resumix Extracts Skills

Here's a look at how the skills extracted from the resume might be listed in this applicant's skills bucket:

> Project Leadership, Software Engineering and Analysis, Computer Application Development, Research and fact finding, Oracle Developer 2000, Software Engineering Specifications Preparation

Skills extraction is the most valuable feature of the Resumix resume in employers' eyes, since it saves them the time and trouble of sorting through stacks of resumes to decide who would be best qualified for what job.

And because it's the most valuable feature to employers, it has to be the most important to you, the applicant. You have to understand that, in a sense, all you are to Resumix is a collection of skills, and all job openings are, to Resumix, a summary of skills written in the Position Descriptions. You want to make sure that your skills match the skills that make up the job you want. We will analyze vacancy announcements and position descriptions in Part 3.

In Parts 4 and 5 we'll give you the step-by-step approach to writing an electronic resume to help you focus on nouns, verbs, knowledge, skills abilities, accomplishments, and plain language — all language that matches the general grammar. This clear, complete and concise writing style will maximize the chances that you'll be matched up with the job you want. For now, here's another look at how skills extraction creates your skills bucket.

How can a computer program like Resumix know what a skill is?

Resumix uses artificial intelligence to figure out what skills you have.

The programmers at the Resumix company first created the program to help employers match applicants to jobs. Since then, the programmers have "taught" (programmed) the software to recognize 40,000 skills — everything from "personnel supervision" to "Oracle database management" to "financial statement auditing."

Furthermore, the programmers have taught Resumix to understand English grammar well enough to recognize skills even if they are written in several different ways. One computer specialist could say in her resume that she *maintained databases;* another could say she was *in charge of database maintenance;* and another could say she *performed maintenance of main-frame DB2 and other databases.* Resumix would recognize any of those as the skill "database maintenance."

Resumix programmers also realized that some employers require employees with special skills. So the programmers enabled employers to add additional skills — their local grammar — to the program's intelligence. That, obviously, is important for the Defense Department. HR offices throughout Defense can add skills to the Resumix skills list that are specific to their needs. So, for example, an employer at the Pentagon can add "Future Year Defense Program Information System" knowledge to the Resumix skills list.

Sample Skills Bucket and Analysis

Here is a resume we will analyze for skills. Susan Gaines entire electronic resume is in the appendix of the book and on the CD-ROM.

SUSAN GAINES

Skills include: Office work, clerical expertise, office management, catering, and gourmet food preparation, food management and ordering, customer satisfaction.

Susan has been a secretary since 1990. She also worked with her family construction business. She owned and operated a catering business previously. She has gone back to school to finish her B.A. in Business and is a GS-5 Secretary now trying to upgrade her job series in government. She would like to be considered for a position as Program Assistant, Administrative Assistant or Management Assistant where she can use her college courses and her business skills.

Susan's skills bucket is printed in this chapter. You will notice the "Categories" field at the top of her skills bucket. It says CLERICAL. That was not Susan's goal. She wanted her resume to be classified as ADMINISTRATIVE.

What's wrong with Susan's skills bucket?

Susan's skills bucket is NOT focused on the skill words for Administrative Assistant, Program Assistant, or Management Assistant. It is filled with a collection of words — college course titles, general job description language, and a few words that are not supportive of her government career objectives. For instance, here is a list of words and descriptions that should not have taken up valuable skills bucket space:

Restaurant management skills: Her small catering business was evidently described in detail and too many irrelevant words have hit her skills bucket, such as cooking, restaurant, vinyl, recipe, food cost control, retailing, and enhancing sales.

Clerical skills: Too many clerical terms in this resume have landed in the skills bucket, such as correspondence, data entry, filing, mail sorting, typing, and office automation.

College course titles: Too many college course titles in this skills bucket are not relevant to her new objective. They took up valuable skills bucket space that should have been used for language from work experience sections.

Valuable Skills Bucket "Real Estate" Lessons

Do not include any words that you do not want to be in your skills bucket. The system will extract them and put them in your bucket.

Select career-focused language. Susan's skills bucket does not include the following skills which could have been helpful to her career-change objective, such as research, analysis, writer, editor, skills, project coordinator, planner, problem-solver, decisions, cooperate, supervisor, liaison, administrator, organizer, trainer, assistant, system designer, management advisor, and technical assistant.

Nouns are the best searchable terms/skills. Almost every noun will be a hit for your skills bucket. Select each carefully. You will see many nouns and verbs used in the samples in the CD-ROM.

You will read much more about how to write in a more concise way with more meaningful words (nouns and verbs) in Part 4 (Writing Your Resume) and Part 5 (Editing and Formatting Tips).

Beware of acronyms. They may not be searchable terms. Acronyms and special terms may not be in the local grammar and they will definitely not be in the general grammar. Spell the name out and then include the acronym in parentheses if you want to use it later.

Write technical information more than one way. For example, if you are a helicopter repairman, include the type of helicopter you repair, but also write "helicopter repairman."

Length of resume: The Navy, Marines, and Air Force resume length is up to five pages at 12-point type with one-inch margins. It's possible that the 199 skills will be extracted in the first 3 1/2 pages. Include your most important skills and descriptions within your Work Experience, Training, and Other information in the first 3 1/2 pages. The Army format is only three pages, so your skills will be extracted from all three pages.

Why allow five pages if the skills won't be extracted? If you are found qualified through skills extraction, then a hiring manager receives your five-page paper resume. The full history of your career will be there if you choose to write this length. The most important and needed information and experience in your career is within the last five to ten years! Any prior experience that is applicable to your new job expectations can be listed as Prior Experience.

Average electronic resume length: Three pages! Don't push yourself to write five pages of text. Most resumes are three pages in length.

The Magic Skills vs. 199 Skills: You do not have to have 199 skills to be successful with a search. You just need to have the four to six magic skills in your bucket! The magic skills are the searchable terms that a hiring manager will select for a search. For example, an employer searched three skill terms recently so that she would get a higher number of resumes from her search. None of her three searchable terms were acronyms or local grammar because she wanted candidates from private industry. She was casting her net for the broadest possible opportunity.

The magic searchable skills: No one knows what the searchable skills are for the various occupations. You have to write a resume that includes your knowledge, skills and abilities, qualifications and accomplishments. Envision the words likely to be in your Skills Bucket. How focused can you make your Skills Bucket?

OFFICIAL LIST OF SKILLS AND MAGIC SKILLS. There is no such thing. If the skill titles were available to you, the system would not work. It's up to you to write a good resume with your knowledge, skills, and abilities. The time invested in research and good writing will pay off in your career.

BOTTOM LINE: Write your resume carefully. Research the industry language for your occupations; do not waste space with unnecessary words; focus on the first three pages and Work Experience descriptions — all of which is thoroughly described in Part 4 in this book. Susan Gaines' entire Resumix resume is in the appendix of the book.

Sample Skills Bucket

Susan A. Gaines

Categories: Clerical, Administrative

Skills:

Teaching	Performance Awards	Leadership Program
Leadership	Total Quality Mgmt	DOS
Microcomputers	Hypertext	HTML
Business Mgmt	Medical Secretarial	Legal Experience
QuickBooks	Math Equations	Algebra
Psychology	Network	Telecomm Exp
Data Communications	DBMS	Economics
Public Speaking	System Design	Systems Analysis
Statistics	Academic Honors	Information Tech/IS
Computer System	Accounting Exp	Enhance Sales
Restaurant	Federal Tax	Purchase Equipment
Material Ordering	Billing	Food Cost Control
Recipe	Cooking	Sales Experience
Retailing	Bookkeeping	Office Management

Rental Management	Cost Analysis	Vinyl
Commodity Resin	Tax ReturnTaxes	Income Tax
IRS Form W-2	Vendor	P&L Statement
Profit & Loss	Cost Control	Cost Estimation
Estimating	Contractual Terms	Contract Development
Proposal Writing	Contract Complexity	Oceanography
Reorganization	Meeting Planning	Voucher
Travel Arrangements	Classified Docs	Distribute Material
Appointments	Time Card	Document Production
Supervision	Satellite	Data Entry
Expenses	Freedom of Info	Privacy Act
Document Prep	Job Description	Correspondence
Employee Recognition	Insurance	Health Insur Prog
Payroll	Payroll Processing	Strategic Planning
Process Action Team	Team-Player	Memo of Agreement
Typing	Proofreading	Mail Sorting
Document Distribution	Logistics	Quality Ctrl
Database Mgmt	World Wide Web	Customer Base
Military Experience	RFP	Receiving
Space Center	Secretarial	Written Communication
Oral Communication	Communication Skills	Ability to Listen
Creative	Adaptable	Industrious
Professionalism	Customer Needs	Writing Skills
Assembly Experience	Analytical Ability	Problem Solving
Accomplishments	Hearing Disabled	Employee Assistance
Policies & Procedures	Filing	Office Automation
Database	Geog Source Prep	Mailing List
Storage & Retrieval	Edit Writing	UNIX
Programming	Basic	Formatting
Internet	Lotus 123	Spreadsheet
Excel	WordPerfect	dBase
MS PowerPoint	Harvard Graphics	MS Access

Word Processing	Microsoft Word	Microsoft Office
MS Windows	Training Experience	Staff Education
Customer Satisfaction	Prod & Services Quality	Customer Service
Construction Work	Financial Management	Financial Experience
Small/Disadvantaged	Small Business	Work Independently
Self-Motivated	*Computer Literate	Workers Compensation

Work History

1993	Present	Financial Manager	Gaines Construction Co.
5/2000	Present	Secretary	Warfighting Support
7/1997	5/2000	Secretary	Warfighting Support
1/1995	7/1997	Secretary	Warfighting Support

Chapter Review

The words that you use in your resume will become your Skills Bucket. Do not include words that you DO NOT WANT extracted into your skills bucket. Remember that the first three pages are the most important skills bucket pages. Use more nouns and verbs. Think about the magic words that describe your experience and skills. Research industry terminology. Study Chapters 8 and 9 in this book to learn how to search for the current descriptions of work.

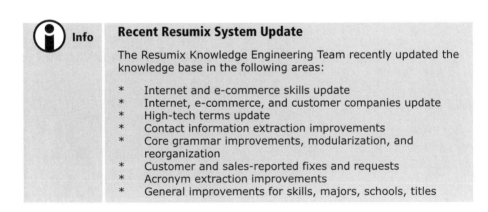

(i) Info   **Recent Resumix System Update**

The Resumix Knowledge Engineering Team recently updated the knowledge base in the following areas:

* Internet and e-commerce skills update
* Internet, e-commerce, and customer companies update
* High-tech terms update
* Contact information extraction improvements
* Core grammar improvements, modularization, and reorganization
* Customer and sales-reported fixes and requests
* Acronym extraction improvements
* General improvements for skills, majors, schools, titles

Looking for good management keywords?

Daniel Goleman writes about collaboration, teamwork, and the group mind in *Working with Emotional Intelligence* (Bantam Trade, 2000). Managers in today's government agencies are managing change through people. How can you write about this? How can leadership and management be best described to maximize hits in the skills bucket and elicit the best reaction from a hiring manager? Goleman's book provides valuable help when you write about complex management challenges and teamwork.

Here are a few important keywords for managers from Goleman's book: teamwork, performance levels, team performance, building bonds, collaboration and cooperation, team capabilities, build rapport, cultivate informal networks, connections, balance a focus on tasks, relationship manager, respect, helpfulness, cooperation, enthusiastic participation, build team identity, esprit de corps, commitment, and share credit.

Chapter 3

Job Kits Made Easier

"Follow the directions!"

From the Army to the Navy to the Air Force to the Defense Finance and Accounting Service Kansas City, we asked hiring officials for advice to pass on to you, the job applicant.

Personnelist after personnelist gave the same answer as the most important piece of advice: "Follow the directions!"

But when we asked people who tried to apply for jobs about their experiences, the most common complaint was, "I can't understand the directions."

That's why we wrote this chapter.

This entire chapter with four of the Job Kits Made Easier are on the CD-ROM. You will want to access the Web site addresses online when you are analyzing job kits and preparing to submit your resume.

Step-by-Step Guide

When you're ready to dive into the applicant pool, open up this chapter for a step-by-step guide, written in plain English. When you're ready to create the electronic resume that you'll use to apply for jobs at the major Defense Department organizations, consider this chapter your personal guide. It will hold your hand through the application process and give you the peace of mind that you did it right.

Everyone wonders why the Federal hiring process is so difficult. Why are there 20-page job kits with job application instructions, when in private industry, you simply send in a resume and letter and the application is done? I don't know the answer, but I do know how to help you understand the new automated processes. Once you understand the resume, the resume builder, and vacancy announcement terms, the process will become clearer. Please be patient and read these chapters. The samples on the CD-ROM will also be wonderful guides as you begin to write your resume.

A word about job kits: Most Defense Department organizations use the term "job kit" to describe the directions they've written for applicants. This chapter is called "Job Kits Made Easier" because we think the application process can be very challenging. In this chapter, we've simplified the job kits down to the basics. In this chapter, we review the critical elements from the job kits provided by the Navy and Marines (page 70), Air Force (page 59), Army (page 62), Defense Finance and Accounting Service — Kansas City (page 66).

They Are All Different

A job applicant wrote and asked questions about submitting her resume to an agency's database. The first questions I asked her were: *Which database? Which agency? What region?* You will see from the analysis of four Job Kits and four agency HR operations that they are all different. Some agencies have "inventory-building, open-continuously" announcements to which you submit your resume and wait for e-mails saying you are qualified for a job (like Monster.com and other online resume posting services).

Other agencies have inventory-building announcements, plus specific job announcements with closing dates for which you have to "self-nominate." If you don't self-nominate, you will not be considered. To be considered for employment with these agencies, you still have to watch the announcements and self-nominate.

There is a mixed bag of uses for the automated systems. That does make this system challenging. That's why this book includes so much information about "how to apply" and job kit analysis, in addition to resume writing. You can write a great resume, but if you can't understand how to apply, it won't do you any good. We're here to help job applicants with both areas — how to apply and how to write a good electronic resume.

Critical Job Questions

Here's what you need to look for when you are considering applying to a particular agency:

1. What is the page length requirement for this agency's HR office?

2. Are the vacancy announcements "Inventory Building" or "real" or both? Look at the closing dates. If the closing date is two years away, it's an inventory-building announcement.

3. Do you submit the resume and wait for e-mails or do you "self-nominate or both?

4. Are their announcements open to the public or internal only?

5. Do they have a Delegated Examining Unit (hiring from the outside) or are they just Merit Promotion (internal hires only)?

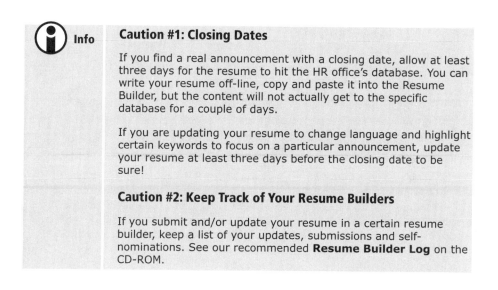

Info

Caution #1: Closing Dates

If you find a real announcement with a closing date, allow at least three days for the resume to hit the HR office's database. You can write your resume off-line, copy and paste it into the Resume Builder, but the content will not actually get to the specific database for a couple of days.

If you are updating your resume to change language and highlight certain keywords to focus on a particular announcement, update your resume at least three days before the closing date to be sure!

Caution #2: Keep Track of Your Resume Builders

If you submit and/or update your resume in a certain resume builder, keep a list of your updates, submissions and self-nominations. See our recommended **Resume Builder Log** on the CD-ROM.

Who Can Apply for DOD Jobs?

It's surprising that most government jobs are not open to everyone. Most government jobs require that you have some kind of "status" with the government. Status commonly refers to individuals among the public who fall in one (or more) of the following categories:

* eligible for reinstatement (worked for the government before)

* eligible for a VRA or VEOA appointment

* 30% disabled veterans

* afflicted with a disability and are eligible for appointment under special hiring authorities

But now some government and almost all the major DOD agencies hire people who do not have status. Some human resources offices have special hiring operations called Delegated Examining Units (DEUs) where they recruit and select people with no status.

The other method of hiring — 90% of all agencies — is through promoting from within, entitled Merit Promotion. This is the traditional way that agencies consider current employees for possible promotion. There are two categories of people who can apply and receive consideration:

* current Federal employees of the agency issuing the vacancy announcement

* individuals who are not current employees, but who do have "status"

If you are a member of the general public, and you do not have "status" under one of these options, you cannot apply and cannot receive consideration.

Under the Delegated Examining Unit, any member of the general public with U.S. citizenship can apply and receive consideration, regardless of whether or not he or she has status. Delegated examining is a service formerly provided exclusively by OPM local area offices. OPM still is a provider of this kind of hiring, but over the last five to ten years, OPM has delegated this hiring authority to the agencies.

When you are reading the Job Kit instructions and the vacancy announcements, be aware of who can apply:

* **Merit Promotion** (internal only)

* **Status Required** (internal or a special hiring authority)

* **Open to Anyone** (internal or external candidates — DEU)

Section Review

Overall, if you focus on one agency and one job kit at a time, and submit your resume correctly, you will be successful with your job search. The new system is more effective than the old system, but remember there is a learning curve for applicants. Those applicants who write a good resume with the right words and get their resumes into databases, will be considered for many jobs. OK, ready? Let's dive in…

Job Kit Made Easier: AIR FORCE CIVILIAN JOBS

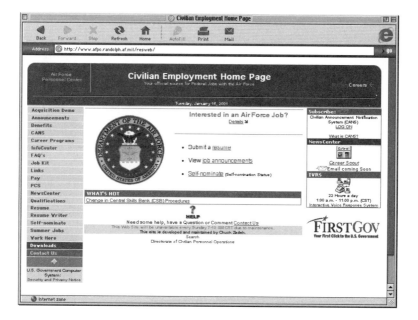

http://www.afpc.randolph.af.mil/resweb/

* *Air Force Civilian Employment News*: Keep informed of the latest recruitment and job placement processes within Air Force by reading the Career Scout from the following page:

    http://www.afpc.randolph.af.mil/resweb/news/news.htm

How to Apply

* Positions and employees covered by Air Force Career Programs. The Air Force Civilian Career Programs provide a centralized merit promotion system used to fill senior management posi tions throughout the Air Force. A brief statistical overview of the 17 programs is available at:

http://www.afpc.randolph.af.mil/cp/contact.htm

A. Current Career Program Registrants:

http://www.afpc.randolph.af.mil/resweb/csb.htm

* Must register in specific career programs to compete for vacancies. Visit the Air Force Career Program home page at http://www.afpc.randolph.af.mil/cp/ to review qualification criteria.

* Skill codes and various ranking factors are utilized to rank candidates.

* Resume and self-nomination may be used to fill specific positions (scientific and engineering series). Carefully review each program's job application requirements.

B. Current DOD Civil Service employees:

* Positions that are designated hard-to-fill will be advertised to all DOD employees at Office of Personnel Management (OPM) Web site http://www.usajobs.opm.gov

* Resumix resume requirements (http://www.afpc.randolph.af.mil/resweb/) may be required and any specific requirements noted in the announcement.

* Non-Federal and Non-DoD candidates are sometimes not eligible.

Positions not covered by Air Force Career Programs and offered through the Delegated Examining Unit (DEU).

All external applicants are required to submit a resume as outlined in the AFPC Job Kit and then self-nominate for job announcements, either through our Civilian Employment Web Site or by calling our Interactive Voice Response System (IVRS), at 1-800-699-4473 (within area code (210) 527-2377).

How to apply: Submit a Resumix resume plus self-nominate. Do not submit a new resume for each announcement. The automated applicant supply file system (Resumix) can continuously maintain your resume. Once you submit a resume and it is on file all you need to do is self-nominate.

Vacancy Announcements

http://www.afpc.randolph.af.mil/resweb/location9a.asp

* Vacancies will be announced and advertised on the Air Force Personnel Centers Employment Home Page

www.afpc.randolph.af.mil/afjobs

* Vacancy listings will also be accessible through our Interactive Voice Response System (IVRS) by calling 1-800-997-2378 (within area code (210) 527-2378). The vacancy listing will be updated each Friday. (Comment: This will not list all AF job vacancies)

CANS — vacancy announcements by e-mail!

* Open Candidate Announcement Notification System (CANS) can be found at http://www.afpc.randolph.af.mil/resweb/cans.htm. Sign up to receive vacancy announcements based on a short questionnaire that you will complete. You can then "Self-Nominate" for positions that are of interest to you. This will save you searching time for vacancy announcements.

* Self-nomination: Yes, for some positions by some applicants.

https://www.afpc.randolph.af.mil/resweb/cans.htm

Where is the Resume Writer?

https://www.afpc.randolph.af.mil/resweb/resume/resume-writer.htm

* Follow the instructions for Internal vs. External use of the Resume Writer

* Resume updating? Anytime, use the Resume Writer with your password

* Resources for keywords

http://www.afpc.randolph.af.mil/resweb/education.htm

* Click on Qualifications. Read position descriptions and Core Documents, which will give you keywords and qualifications required for Air Force positions.

Job Kit Made Easier: ARMY CIVILIAN JOBS

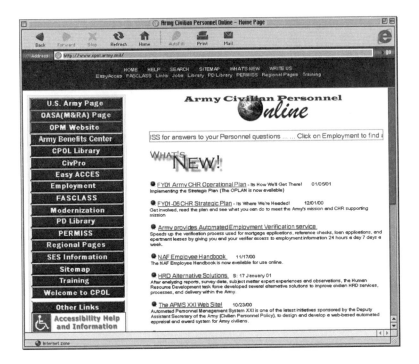

Web site: www.cpol.army.mil

* Resume length: 2 pages for Europe and West regions
  3 pages for all other regions

* Databases:10

* Regions: 10

How to Apply

* Resume Builder
* E-mail — do not send attached files
* Hard copy by mail.
* Vacancy Announcements: Open continuously, specific closing dates
* Self-nomination: Yes, for some announcements

Where is the Resume Builder?

www.cpol.army.mil

Background

* Army Civilian Training Offices are approximately 50% deployed with Resumix/STAIRS and the use of the Resume Builder. Many announcements still require KSAs and paper applications.

Vacancy Announcements and Instructions

* The Army vacancy announcements vary greatly in their "how to apply" instructions. Just follow the directions.

Example # 1 — US Army Engineering Research and Development Center, Champlain, IL (the Old Way!)

HOW TO APPLY: All applicants must complete and sign the attached Supplemental Qualification Statement (SQS). Applicants must provide two (2) sets of copies of their signed SQS and SF171, OF612, DA Form 2302, or resume and a copy of their most recent performance appraisal when applying against this announcement. Applications WILL NOT not be accepted by fax or E-mail. NOTE: Do NOT use the Resume Builder button provided below to submit your resume. RESUMIX WILL NOT be used to fill these vacancies. ELECTRONIC APPLICATIONS WILL NOT BE ACCEPTED.

Example # 2 Aberdeen, MD (the New Way!)

HOW TO APPLY: Your Resumix resume should already be in the database; Self-Nominate for this position. If you wait to the last minute to submit your resume to the Resume Builder, it may not get to the Civilian Training Operation Center (CPOC) in time. It's best to put the resume into the database early, then look for an announcement and self-nominate.

If you are currently serviced by the Northeast Civilian Personnel Operation Center, you must have a resume on file with our office to self-nominate. Employees may submit a resume at any time; however, we cannot guarantee the resume will be processed by the closing date of the announcement. If you are submitting your resume in response to this announcement, please note you will also need to include your self-nomination. For assistance, you may contact your local Civilian Personnel Advisory Center.

To self-nominate, give your Name; SSN; Announcement Number; Position Title, Pay Plan, Series, Grade of the Position you are applying for; Work and/ or Home Telephone Numbers; lowest acceptable grade/salary; and typing and/or steno dictation speed words per minute (if applicable). If the position has a mandatory education requirement, please certify as to whether you meet the requirement and how. See Where to Submit Package for self-nomination address.

Research

Army's PD Library

Search Capabilities: This page provides vacancy announcement searching for six employment categories:

* Morale/Welfare & Recreation Jobs

* Reserve Military Technician Jobs

* Entry Level "Civilian Careers" Non-Clerical

* Hard-to-Fill Medical Positions (no previous Federal experience required)

* Career Program Positions- normally GS 13, 14, 15.

Seventeen jobs were available: Ten were "inventory-building" announcements; seven were real jobs.

Resume Builder: INSTRUCTIONS LINK

* Read this information! It is important! Better print these out and read thoroughly before filling out the Resume Builder.

* FILL OUT REQUIRED FIELDS BEFORE YOU CAN SAVE

* The red asterisks have to be completed before you can save.

* **Update**? You must update your resume every 90 days.

Say What?

Three page length means: 12-point type, Times, One inch margins. See formats in CD-ROM.

Inside Scoops

Army CPOL Offices for Europe and West require two-page resumes; all other ARMY regions will allow three pages.

Pet Peeve

ONE RESUME ONLY! One Army personnelist told us that applicants keep submitting resumes, even after they already have the applicant's resume from a previous submission. You only need to send your resume to each database one time, then SELF-NOMINATE with a simple e-mail.

Job Kit Made Easier:
DEFENSE FINANCE AND ACCOUNTING SERVICE-
KANSAS CITY, DELEGATED EXAMINING UNIT, KS

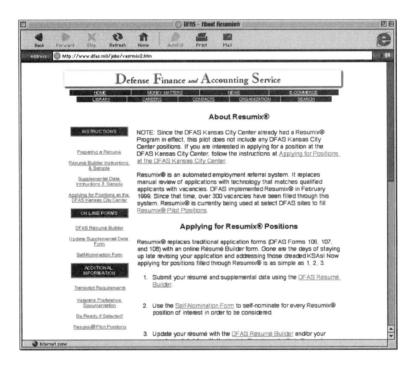

Web site: www.dfas.mil/people/kcdeu/

* Resume length: Up to 3 pages

* Databases: The DEU has its own applicant database

How to Apply

* The online resume builder is preferred

* E-mail — do not send attached files; place resume text in the text box.

* Fax — not preferred

* Hardcopy by mail (use Job Kit format)

* Vacancy Announcements can be found at:

  http://www.dfas.mil/jobs/

* There are no closing dates on announcements.

* All jobs are posted for applicants to study and submit resumes into databases for future candidate searches.

* Self-nomination for jobs? No, for the Kansas City databases

Where is the Resume Builder?

* The Resume Builder link is inside the vacancy announcement and on the Web site.

* Resume Updating: Applicants can submit a new or updated resume at any time for each announcement if desired. The resume will be considered for multiple Vacancy Announcements.

Vacancy Announcements

* Locations: Go to www.dfas.mil/people/kcdeu/ or check the OPM USAJOBS website (look by individual job series)

* Most vacancy announcements are open indefinitely; others are published on an "as needed" basis and have specific closing dates.

* All jobs are posted for applicants to study and submit resumes into the database for future candidate searches.

* Where is the Resume Builder? The Resume Builder link can be

found inside DEU announcements on OPM USAJOBS or on the DEU web site.

* Resume Updating: Applicants can submit a new or updated resume at any time for each open announcement, if desired. A separate resume must be submitted for each announcement for which consideration is desired. Each resume has an active life limited to 90 days. To receive additional consideration beyond 90 days under specific announcements, applicants must submit a new resume.

Background

The DFAS Kansas City site is home to the DFAS Delegated Examining Unit. The site also maintains its own separate and distinct merit promotion candidate inventory for filling local positions. KC has been using the Resumix system since August 1996. KC was one of the early DOD locations to fully implement Resumix and has been very successful with its instructions and selection processes. The Kansas City internal merit promotion program is a true database - like Monster.com. Merit promotion vacancy announcements for vacant Kansas City site positions can be found at www.dfas.mil/jobs/. Specific application procedures to receive consideration for Kansas City site merit promotion vacancies can be found at www.dfas.mil/jobs/resume/ DFAS-KC.htm. There are two Job Kits accessible from this page, one for current KC employees and one for all other external applicants. You can also find them on the CD-ROM, Applying for Employment with the Federal Government. Instructions for applying for consideration for positions advertised through the DFAS Delegated Examining Unit can be found at www.dfas.mil/people/kcdeu/DeuHowToApply.htm.

Research

* Glossary of Common Terms at DFAS

  http://www.dfas.mil/jobs/vasgen.htm#glossary of terms

* Other Noteworthy Features of the DFAS DEU Website

* Job Opportunities — Description of Federal Occupations

  http://www.dfas.mil/people/kcdeu/DeuJobAnnouncements.htm

Resume Builder and Resume Writing Instructions

* Sample Resume

  http://www.dfas.mil/people/kcdeu/DeuSampleResume.htm

* Two accounting resumes are posted with excellent analysis of what's good and what's not.

* How to Prepare an Effective Resume for Electronic Analysis and Evaluation

  http://www.dfas.mil/people/kcdeu/DEUResumePreparation.htm

* This is SUPERB RESUME WRITING INSTRUCTION!

* You must print and read this information!

* Adapting to a Changing Environment

  http://www.dfas.mil/people/kcdeu/DEUResumePreparation.htm#change

* How does the DEU Automated Resume Processing System Work?

  http://www.dfas.mil/people/kcdeuDEUResumePreparation.htm#process

Pet Peeve

When writing your resume include only job information that will directly contribute to your objective. If your goal is to become a GS-545-8 military pay technician, it is unnecessary to outline experience you had ten years ago as a GS-3 clerk-typist.

Inside Scoop

The DFAS Delegated Examining Unit Job application web site is surprisingly the most applicant-friendly of the four web sites made easy here in this book. The resume-writing instructions are almost as good as what is in this book.

Job Kit Made Easier:
NAVY/MARINES CIVILIAN JOBS

http://www.donhr.navy.mil ... then Jobs, Jobs, Jobs

* Resume length: Up to 5 pages (additional data sheet answers are not part of these 5 pages)

* Databases: 8

* 8 Human Resources Service Centers. Each center fills positions occurring in its geographic region. Announcements and "how to apply" instructions are different for each of the various regions.

How to Apply

* The Department of the Navy online resume builder is preferred.

* Application Express (aka Self-Nomination). Once you have a current resume on file with a Human Resources Service Center, you may be able to use this resume to apply for other announcements issued by this center using the Application Express process.

* E-mail (use Job Kit format). Do not send attached files; place resume in email text. Be sure to answer all Additional Data Sheet questions.

* Hardcopy by mail (use Job Kit format). Be sure to answer all Additional Data Sheet questions.

Vacancy Announcements

* Open until filled; and individual one-time announcements with specific closing dates.

* Application Express/Self-nomination: Yes. A self-nomination link (Application Express) will be added to each vacancy announcement in the near future.

Where is the Resume Builder/Application Express?

* Resume Builder and Application Express buttons can be found at the end of those announcements that allow for these application methods.

Additional Data Sheet

* Can be found at the end of the Resume Builder.

* Different for each Human Resources Service Center.

Resume Updating

* You can update as often as you like. Your most recent resume on file with a Human Resources Service Center is the resume of record used when applying using the Application Express process.

Background

*   Navy/Marines are almost 100% deployed with Resumix/ STAIRS (Standard Automated Inventory and Referral System) and the use of the Navy Resume Builder.

Employment Information

*   Job Opportunities

    Access www.donhr.navy.mil. Click on Job Opportunities.

Vacancy Announcements

*   See the Job Opportunities by Title or Region

*   Jobs, Jobs, Jobs to see a map of the Navy's 8 regions

    Access www.donhr.navy.mil. Click on Job Opportunities and then Jobs, Jobs, Jobs.

This page has a colorful map linked to each of the Navy's regions. Since each region has a separate application database, you must submit a separate resume under an individual vacancy announcement for each of the regions you want consideration for. Keep a list of where you have submitted your resume. See a sample Resume Region/Database Log in the CD-ROM.

Research

Three ways to search for jobs:

1. Search All Open Positions to find the job titles for which you are qualified and would like to be considered by hiring managers.

2. Search by Region by using the colorful map. Note that many regions also issue vacancy announcements for geographic areas serviced by other regions. So vacancies for San Diego may be filled by the Southwest and Northwest regions.

3. Search by Job Title for all regions.

Resume Builder Instructions

* Open with your Social Security No. and case sensitive Pass word. Do not forget your password.

* Work Experience Instructions

  http://www.donhr.navy.mil/resume/workexp.html

* Your Work Experience description fields can be up to 7,700 characters.

* Scroll all the way to the end of the announcement to find a link to the on-line builder. Insert your password and user name (write them down). Complete all of the red questions before you can save your resume builder information. You can return to work on your resume, then hit SUBMIT to actually submit the resume to the region's human resource office.

Inside Scoop

UNANNOUNCED JOB SEARCHES WORK! Many of the jobs in the U.S. Navy and U.S. Marines database are posted on the database and listed as "Open until Filled." These announcements are building an inventory of interested and qualified candidates for "Unannounced Job Searches."

Say What?

When you create and submit your resume in the Navy resume builder it is saved on a central webserver maintained in San Antonio, Texas and then forwarded to specific region that issued the vacancy announcement .

If you want your resume to be on file in different regions, you have to apply to a vacancy announcement for each region where you wish consideration.

Part 2
New Automated
Human Resources Methods

Chapter 4

What Happens to Your Resume: Following the Electronic Trail

Since the old way of submitting a separate SF-171, OF-612, and KSA set for every announcement has been replaced by Resume Builders and "one resume" per database, there is an entirely different electronic trail to getting selected. Follow the trail of your electronic resume.

First You Submit Your Resume Through a Resume Builder

Info Each agency and region has its own Resume Builder. Navy has one Resume Builder linked to eight databases in eight regions. Army has ten. Air Force has one. DFAS has two. OPM USAJOBS has one. You might be wondering why there are so many resume builders and databases. Because each human resources office wants control of its own resumes and vacancy announcements.

Most Resume Builders are similar. Once you have submitted your resume one time, the second time will be easier. Before your resume can leave your computer, you have to write it, and then you have to figure out where and how to post it. It's helpful to know the process that it will follow after you hit "submit." Where does it go?

First, here's what you have to do to get the resume on the trail toward being "selected" for your next job.

1. Find the Web site for the agency you would like to consider.

2. Find at least one vacancy announcement on the agency's Web site that will support your career objectives.

3. Find the Resume Builder and Job Kit of the agency (or agencies) that interest you. Read the instructions. These Web pages are in Chapter 3, "Job Kits Made Easier" and on the CD-ROM.

4. Review the requirements for the particular Resume Builder you are using. Note specifications that are listed. These often include number of allowable pages, acceptable type fonts, font size, symbols to avoid, and use of acronyms.

5. Answer the questions on the Additional Data Sheet carefully. These will be found at the end of the Resume Builder.

6. Write your resume offline in a word processing system.

7. Spellcheck, edit, and then have someone read the resume who does not work with you to see if he or she understands it.

8. Review the Resume Builder submission procedures. You can usually complete some of the resume, save what you've completed, and then return to finish and submit.

9. Enter the information into the required fields, using copy and paste to transfer your text file into the corresponding sections in the Resume Builder.

10. If there is a preview button in the Resume Builder, click on this feature to view the information entered and how it will appear. When you have completed all your entries and are satisfied that it meets the specifications of the particular Resume Builder, save the document and print out a copy of what will be entered into the system.

11. Your final step is to submit the resume to the human resources database. You can simply click submit in your Resume Builder and it will be received by the region where the vacancy announcement has been produced. You will receive an e-mail notification that your resume has been successfully submitted and accepted into the system.

12. Keep track of your resume builder submittals by keeping a Resume Builder Log. See the Chart in this chapter. A template for this chart is on the CD-ROM. If you do not remember where you posted your resume, you could lose valuable time when you could be submitting resumes for newly posted announcements.

The vacancy announcement will also specify if other means of submission are acceptable. For example, you may have the option of submitting by e-mail, regular mail, or fax transmission, however, some HR offices will not accept mail or fax. Whichever means of submitting your resume you choose, be sure you follow the steps precisely. If e-mail is acceptable, verify if your resume must be copied and pasted as a text file into the body of the e-mail message and what must be entered into the subject line. Also, determine if there are specifications on acceptable word processing software systems and versions for any that may accept e-mail attachments. Be aware that some human resources offices do not accept e-mail attachments.

Second, Here's What the Human Resource Office Will Do

1. A computer operator (personnel) will receive your resume by e-mail and review your resume for the existence and accuracy of basic, required information (your name, e-mail, phones, address, and answers to the additional data sheet). Once verified, the resume becomes active in the electronic system. You will receive an e-mail stating that your resume was successfully submitted to the database.

2. Each applicant has an individual electronic file that contains the resume text and a resume summary section. Your resume turns into a "skills bucket," which is a list of keywords that represent your Knowledge, Skills, and Abilities (KSAs), education and/or training, and experience extracted from the resume by the software.

3. When a job opening occurs, a human resources recruiter accesses the skills bucket of each applicant on file (in some cases, for applicants who have self-nominated) and compares its contents with the keywords and KSAs identified for successful performance in the vacant job.

Third, the Hiring Manager's Request to Recruit

1. The selecting official provides the Human Resource Office (HRO) with the position description (PD) for the vacant job. Or the hiring manager writes the PD with the help of the HRO.

2. The HRO uses the PD to perform a job analysis to identify KSAs present in the position.

3. The selecting official and HRO jointly review the results of the job analysis to decide which keys or significant KSAs are essential for satisfactory performance on the job.

4. Both parties then review the knowledge base to designate the same or comparable KSAs for inclusion in a search. They come up with a list of keywords for searching the occupational series or self-nominated candidates.

Fourth, HRO's Search and Match Process

1. HRO recruiters begin to review applicant skills buckets for the presence of appropriate KSAs, keywords and qualifications.

2. When the search phase is completed (in a matter of seconds), the screen displays a list of potential candidates in rank order based on the total number of designated KSAs found in their skills buckets. This completes the rating and ranking process.

3. Staffing specialists then review the resumes of the top ranked candidates to insure the presence of necessary specialized experience, appropriate quality of experience, required time-in-grade (if applicable), or possession of substitutable education. All of these factors determine if candidates meet minimum qualification criteria. (Read Chapter 5, "Getting Qualified" for more information on qualifications.) This minimum qualification phase has no impact on candidates' scores or rankings already assigned by the HR system.

4. Top-ranked candidates meeting minimum qualification require ments are referred to the selecting official for consideration for possible selection and employment. The HRO will try to send 10 to 15 candidates for each recruitment.

5. If you are one of the top-ranked, qualified candidates, you will receive notification that you are qualified and are being referred for consideration. You should respond by indicating whether or not you are interested and available for the position.

Fifth, the Hiring Manager's Decision and the Job Interview

1. The hiring manager will receive a printout copy of your resume that was put into the resume builder. They will read the resume and review your overall qualifications. The manager will not be advised of your individual ranking, nor will he or she have access to your skills bucket.

2. The manager will compare your background with those of other referred candidates. A decision will be made on whether or not to contact you for an interview. This is where your accomplishments could really make you stand out.

3. An interview may be conducted in person, by videoconference (Picture-Tel), or telephone. Your ability to communicate verbally will be important in the hiring manager's decision. You will need to distinguish yourself as a communicator, and you should make a concerted effort to "sell" or promote yourself to the selecting official.

4. The selecting manager will make a decision, and hopefully, you will receive an offer of employment.

Solution and Success Recommendations

1. Spend time: Write your resume and focus it on significant skills in your background for a successful search. Cut to the chase: Be concise, but descriptive.

2. Play the game: Submit your resume to multiple resume builders and databases so that you will be in a position to receive maximum consideration.

 **Info**

Well-crafted resumes in multiple databases net qualified candidates the highest frequency of contacts.

Resume Database Log: Keep a log of your resume updates for each of the databases. If you keep your resume in more than one database, you will have to keep track of which resumes you have updated. You will find a template for the Resume Database Log on the CD-ROM. See Chart No. 1 in this chapter.

Chart No. #1 Resume Builder/Database Action Log - Resume Submissions, Self-Nominations, and Udates

Keep track of your resume builder entries with a Resume Database Action Log.

Date	Agency	Region	Annct	Type	Password
11/17/00	Navy	SE	00-00002	Trans. Spec., GS-12 Portsmouth Naval Base, VAInventory	cindy
11/19/00	Army	S	09-00-0000	Logistics Specialist, GS-12 Ft. Belvoir, MD closing date 09/09/00	cindy cindy
11/20/00	Navy	SE	update	closing date10/12/00	
11/23/00	Army	SW	update		
11/24/00	Air Force		09-00-0000	12/31/00	cindy
11/29/00	Air Force		09-00-00	Logistics Mgt., Kelly AFB self nominate	

Chapter Review

The Resume Builder submission, search, rating, raking, and selection process is much faster than the old way of crediting plans, KSAs, and initial staffing reviews. The initial rating and raking now takes seconds. Once you have a good electronic resume that covers your job interests, you will be able to submit your resume to multiple databases — inside and outside of government — and self-nominate as needed for specific vacancy announcements easily. Looking for a new job with the new electronic resume process is easier than the old SF-171, KSA way.

Chapter 5

Getting Qualified: Now the Cream Rises to the Top

How does an applicant get qualified with the new process?

Human Resources offices are using Resumix to search, rate, and rank candidates. They use this software for assistance with any or all of the following:

* To rate and rank all applicants who have selected a specific job series.

* To rate and rank applicants who self-nominate for the specific positions.

* To review for minimum qualifications.

* To forward the resumes to the hiring manager for selection.

No matter which automated processes are being used, two things remain constant:

1. You must be qualified for the job.

2. Your resume must contain the language of the job so that the automated search process extracts it from the masses.

Getting Qualified by a One-Step System

Step 1. Submit your resume for a particular job series.

The Director of the Kansas City Customer Support Unit for the Defense Finance and Accounting Service states that "with the new database development and software queries, the bottom line is that we now focus strictly on potential and experience, and this is the way it should be. A candidate either possesses the requisite knowledge, skills, and abilities in sufficient depth, or he/she does not. A system such as Resumix insures that "the cream rises to the top."

Almost without exception, the ranked lists of candidates provided by Resumix have the best candidates at the top. This type of software simply affords automatic rating and ranking consideration to any employee or outside candidate who has submitted a resume for inclusion in the DFAS Kansas City inventory.

In the past — that is, before Resumix — the process was more complex, with three basic steps in the Merit Promotion process performed in the following order:

1. Reviewing minimum qualifications using OPM Handbook X-118 occupational standards; then

2. Rating and ranking, i.e., assigning "points" based on the possession of KSA factors, and

3. Putting qualified and rated candidates in the proper referral order.

Remember that, in the past, candidates submitted applications in response to specific vacancy announcements. As a result, a DFAS Kansas City staffing specialist performed a manual qualifications review of every single application. Then the applications of those individuals determined to be basically qualified were rated and ranked — also a manual process.

With the advent of Resumix, the processing order has been reversed (at least at the Kansas City location). The Resumix system now electronically performs rating and ranking based on its analysis of KSA factors present in candidate resumes. It provides a ranked list of candidates.

The HR director describes the Kansas City local policy: "We identify the top 15 candidates, including any ties. Staffing specialists then perform a minimum qualifications review on the applications of these candidates. As soon as they have identified the top 15 and tied qualified candidates, no further minimum qualifications reviews are conducted on any remaining, lower-ranking candidates."

Additionally, DFAS in Kansas City does not publish individual, internal vacancy announcements. It does publish open continuous (or inventory building) "blanket" announcements to afford external merit promotion candidates an opportunity to be considered. The normal expiration date for inventory building announcement submission is six months.

The DFAS Kansas City staffing program is "bare bones," designed to minimize the investment of time and labor and to maximize the benefits inherent in automation. "Crediting plans developed for use with Resumix are much easier to compile, easier to understand, and much more straightforward. As a result, the ranking process performed by the system is more accurate and more substantive, thereby generating enhanced candidate quality," states the program director.

Finally, it is easier to refer better-qualified candidates because Resumix performs candidate analysis and subsequent rating and ranking with superior objectivity and unmatched consistency.

Other agencies using the One-Step, Inventory Building System: Some Navy regions. The Navy is searching for candidates with unannounced vacancies in their databases every day. Most private industry online databases are the one-step system. Submit your resume, then wait for e-mails.

Getting Qualified by a Different Two-Step System

Step 1. Submit your resume.

Step 2. Self-nominate for particular positions.

Stephen Janik of the Civilian Personnel Advisory Center (CPAC), Alaska, provides another perspective about the qualification process by Army's Resumix system.

The Army's use of Resumix is different from DFAS Kansas City. The first step is to submit a resume and supplemental data. The second step is to self-nominate for specific positions. The Army system searches only those resumes that have been self-nominated.

Applicants need to focus on making sure they meet minimum eligibility requirements. Many applicants are under the false impression that their resume is rated and basic qualifications are determined by a computer looking for keywords. A personnel specialist is responsible for determining whether an applicant meets legal and regulatory requirements. What Army's Resumix system is designed to do is initially screen the skills of applicants who self-nominate for a position against the skills of the position being filled. The skills match list is used to determine the number of candidates to be referred. Referral lists are created by the software. The South West Civilian Personnel Operations Center (SWCPOC) uses Resumix for storage and retrieval of the applicants' resumes, but not as a qualifications system.

Here's how the review process works with the Army:

1. The Resumix operators send the self-nominated resumes to the staffing specialist.

2. The staffing specialist rates them and determines if the applicant meets legal and regulatory requirements and OPM Qualifications Standards. The staffing specialist also decides if the resume is the correct length and format and contains correct information.

3. Those candidates who are rated qualified are referred to the Civilian Personnel Advisory Center (CPAC), who forwards them to the selecting supervisor. The selecting supervisor then makes hiring decisions.

Other agencies using the Two-Step, Self-Nomination System: U.S. Navy, DFAS Regional Service Center, and Air Force with their Skills Codes database (internal applicants) and the Resumix database (external applicants, as well as internal applicants applying for externally announced positions).

 Info Army, Navy, Marines and Air Force agencies require self-nominations for announcements. For these announcements they will only search for candidates who have self-nominated.

Analyzing Vacancy Announcements for Basic Qualifications

Below are excerpts from two vacancy announcements explaining qualifications requirements. The qualifications information is always located on the vacancy announcement. This is valuable information to review so that you know if you are qualified for a certain position or grade level.

Case Study #1 Secretary (Office Automation) GS 318-05

QUALIFICATION REQUIREMENTS: Applicants must demonstrate possession of one year of specialized experience equivalent to at least the next lower grade level of administrative work, or substitute education as described below. Positions at grade level GS-4 require one year of general experience. Positions at grade level GS-5 and above require one year of specialized experience equivalent to the next lower level in work related to the position to be filled.

A candidate's resume for this position needs to show that he or she has one year of secretarial or equivalent experience immediately below the advertised grade level. The position announcement may not spell out exactly what is required at the next lower grade level.

Case Study #2 Electrical Engineer (all grades) GS 850

QUALIFICATION REQUIREMENTS. A four-year degree qualifies at the GS-5 level. Special Qualifications: all professional engineering positions require a professional engineering degree from an ABET-accredited university.

SPECIALIZED EXPERIENCE: One year of professional experience that has equipped the applicant with the particular knowledge, skills, and abilities (KSAs) to perform successfully in the field of electrical engineering. Once a particular grade level is achieved, each additional year of progressively responsible electrical engineering experience is qualifying for the next higher grade level.

Once the candidate reviews the essential qualifications spelled out in this announcement, he or she needs to apply the correct words within the resume to demonstrate the knowledge, skills, and abilities to perform this job. Using the appropriate words is what triggers the rating and ranking process of the software.

Chapter Review

Each human resources office may be using Resumix in a different way in the process of selecting candidates. Some offices have staffers review candidates' qualifications first while others use the software to search for candidates first.

Find out if you are qualified for a position by reading the Qualification Requirements in the vacancy announcement. Once you know you are qualified, write about your knowledge, skills, and abilities using the language of the position to demonstrate your ability to perform this job, so that you can rise to the top with a computer search.

Pet Peeve

Steve Janik writes this note about multiple resumes:

"One thing about Resumix that is occasionally a problem: The system can only hold one resume per applicant at any one time. When you send in a new resume it replaces the one in the system. The problem comes when people try to tailor their resume toward each vacancy announcement. They will send in a resume, then self-nominate for a vacancy, and then do the same thing over again, not realizing that each time they send in a new resume, the old one disappears.

If you only apply for a job every three or four months you can tailor your resume because the last job you applied for has already been closed out, but when you are applying for a number of vacancies in a short period of time, it can't be done."

Part 3
Research and Career Decision-Making

Chapter 6

Research the Announcements:
Explore the Language for Your Resume

Remember when you were in school and you had to do research for a major paper? The teacher asked for sources on 3 x 5 cards. Well, let's pretend you're back in school and the teacher has given you the assignment to write about your current job, based on industry language and terminology, from at least three outside sources.

The best place to find descriptive sources for your jobs will be vacancy announcements, position descriptions, corporate recruitment advertisements, and mission statements.

As you do your research, it's important to remember why the teacher is asking you to find current sources for writing your work experience descriptions. Remember how the Human Resources recruiters will search for your resume? They will be searching for four to eight keywords that would be typical for a particular occupation in their database. If you want your resume to be "found" in a database, it must be written with the most current terminology.

This chapter is about how to do your research and find the right words to describe your work — for one job or multiple job interests. You can get an A on your paper (resume) if you do your research and follow the instructions in this book on resume writing.

Keywords and KSAs

The CD-ROM with this book includes "Keywords and KSAs" to help you with your research. We analyzed more than 100 occupations and vacancy announcements to pull this list together. The duties and responsibilities were excerpted from the announcement and the keywords were listed.

Here's one example of a vacancy announcement keyword analysis from the CD-ROM:

PROGRAM COORDINATOR

SERIES/GRADE: GS-0301-09/09

HIRING AGENCY: DEPARTMENT OF STATE

DUTY LOCATIONS: WASHINGTON, DC

DUTIES:

Assist the Chairman and Executive Secretaries of the NP/CBM-led missile and CBW licensing working groups. Duties include: recording NP/CBM positions on cases; arranging for and tracking assurances from foreign governments; maintaining database of regime denials; reviewing all licensing against regime denial lists; setting up meetings with industry and foreign governments on licensing issues; responding to inquiries about the status of export cases; sending meeting agendas to group members and helping prepare for meeting; researching and/or analyzing problems, issues or program requirements relating to export control laws, regulations, policies, etc.

Keywords and Skills Extracted

writer	research/analysis	track assurances
set up meetings with industry	regime denials	foreign affairs
meeting planning	status of export cases	researcher
CBW licensing group	foreign governments	export control laws
export regulations	database maintenance	licensing issues

If you find a vacancy announcement that is correct for your job interests, you can continue to do your own research and add more keywords to the list.

Researching Industry Language for Private Industry Job Applicants

When Resume Place writers draft resumes for private industry clients, we always ask clients to provide recruitment advertisements from the Web or newspaper. We also ask for pages from Web sites that describe the company's products or mission. Why do we do that? Because we want to make sure we include the correct terminology and industry language in the resume and cover letter. We've been doing this for 20 years. Looking for the right skill language and keywords is not a new process. Human readers look for keywords — as you know. Federal human resources staff and hiring managers look for keywords and critical skills too!

Teacher Transitions into Corporate Trainer with Industry Language

Recently a teacher of 15 years needed a new resume for her new career goal: corporate training. I asked her to find recruitment ads from major corporations for Corporate Trainer. She found about 25 excellent corporate trainer announcements! They gave me the language that I needed to translate her classroom teaching skills to corporate training. Since my client did some pro bono training with teachers (to foster her career change goals), I was able to truthfully use some of the corporate training language.

Here's how I used some of the corporate training terminology listed in the recruitment ads from training.lucent.com, gpworldwide.com, and Marriott.com.

"Before" Resume as a Classroom Teacher

Trainer, Teacher, Baltimore County Public Schools, Western School of Technology.

Design, create, and implement curriculum, assessments, and behavior programs for Science, Occupational preparation, and English. Edit and proofread papers. Assess and evaluate students. Maintain records and monitor student progress. Train students on use of the Internet and various software applications. Maintain open communication both orally and in writing with parents and team. Conduct team meetings and develop agenda.

"After" Resume with Corporate Trainer Language

Teacher, Western School of Technology   1999 to present

Classroom Teacher and Case Manager

Maryland State Teacher's Association   1998 to 1999

Trainer – Facilitator - Women's Leadership Training

* Professional Training Topics: Educational, including computer skills, Teamwork, DecisionMaking, Accepting Change, Organizational Development, Problem-solving.

* Curriculum designs consider business processes, critical systems, organizational objectives, skills and competency levels

* Materials development: presentation materials, supporting instructional materials, exercises, agenda, course descriptions, marketing and promotional materials

* Technical writing, editing and materials production

* Consult and recommend training solutions to achieve organizational change and corporate/educational goals.

* Strategic planning and communications to achieve training, customer and student learning goals within established schedules and deadlines

* Adaptable and flexible in stand-up teaching environment involving unique teaching situations, travel and unknown variables.

Summary: There's a big difference between the two work experience write-ups because of the industry language.

Systematic Method for Analyzing Vacancy Announcements

Analyzing vacancy announcements can be tedious because of the complex and large volume of information in the announcement. Even so, you have to find the helpful information and disregard the rest.

A favorite lesson in my workshops is a demonstration of my systematic method of analyzing announcements. "Reading an announcement isn't enough," I tell my classes. "You need to read, analyze, and dissect the announcement into sentences and phrases so you can find the keywords."

 Tip "GETTING SELECTED" = RESUME + KEYWORDS FROM VACANCY ANNOUNCEMENTS

Industry Language Search

My systematic method for searching and analyzing industry language follows.

1. Find a Web site where there are recruitment ads or vacancy announcements. Here are a few suggestions:

   www.usajobs.opm.gov

   www.donhr.navy.mil

   www.cpol.army.mil

   www.afpc.randolph.af.mil

   www.msn.com (careers in general)

   You will probably find other Web sites where you can find recruitment advertisements and vacancy announcements in addition to these.

2. Find a recruitment ad or vacancy announcement that includes substantial content describing the job. You will find announcements with lots of good descriptions, and you will find bad announcements with "generic" language. Keep searching for the substantial language.

Here are two examples of announcements for the position of Budget Analyst.

A "Poor" Announcement for Keywords for a Budget Analyst

This series includes all positions, the paramount duties of which are to perform, advise on, or supervise work in any of the phases or systems of budget administration in use in the Federal service, when such work also primarily requires knowledge and skill in the application of related laws, regulations, policies, precedence, methods and techniques of budgeting.

A "Good" Announcement for Keywords for a Budget Analyst

Incumbent performs routine budget administration functions in the formulation, execution, and review of assigned portions of the appropriated fund budget located at the Navy Recruiting District (NRD) Omaha, Nebraska. The incumbent formulates and revises the annual budget estimate for NRD support activities and components (e.g., communications, automated data processing, maintenance, supply, and transportation). Researches, compiles and summarizes data concerning expenses for formulation of budget estimates. Monitors and tracks obligations and expenditures throughout the annual operating budget. Recommends transfer of funds between accounts. Manages all communications systems regarding procurement of equipment, systems, installations, maintenance and payment certifications. Checks the accuracy and adequacy of budget justification data. Prepares data summaries for inclusion and routine and special reports. Drafts procedural guidance to command program managers.

3. Save the good announcement as an HTML document.

4. Open your favorite word processing software program.

5. Copy and paste the Duties and Responsibilities section from the announcement into your favorite word processing program. Also copy and paste any other KSAs or descriptive language from the announcement for further analysis.

6. Enlarge the duties information to 14- or 16-point type for readability.

7. Space out each sentence for easy readability.

8. Edit the words out of the duties section that are not useful (i.e. the incumbent will, responsible for, duties include, tasks include).

9. Print the page out.

10. Underline or highlight words that would appear to be keywords or skills.

Here are two examples of the duties and responsibilities sections of a vacancy announcements — one for a Computer Specialist and one for a Supply Technician — printed out in my systematic method.

Note that this announcement starts out with a great list of nouns. Electronic resumes should include more nouns because they are searchable. (See the Chapter 9 section on "Hats, Nouns, and Skills" to create your resume outline with list of nouns and skills that represent your job.) This is an excellent announcement with a detailed description of the job. There are more than 100 keywords in this announcement. The skill or industry language is italicized.

Announcement Analysis #1, Computer Specialist

Supervisor, subject matter expert, and team leader

Duties & Responsibilities:

Supervisor, subject matter expert, and team leader on a wide variety of automation projects and studies.

Monitor the ongoing *operation of a complex network environment* with a large number of *users* in a 26-state area within the SOUTHDIV AOR.

Analyst performing critical reviews, *test proposals,* and *evaluation plans* to determine impact on and compatibility with the systems architecture.

Author and coordinator of *development* of *system documentation* for complex network and/or telecommunications *assignments* in accordance with DoD, agency, major command, and local standards.

Customers include: influential organizations or organized groups from outside the command.

Negotiator with experience in influencing the commitment of *funding* for NAVFAC-wide automation *acquisitions* or the development of NAVFAC-wide technical *policies/procedures.*

(1) Ability to serve as a *subject matter expert/team leader* and *project manager* on a wide variety of automation projects.

(2) Ability to *implement* new *system hardware* and *software* and develop *operating procedures* for successful *integration* of new technology into the current IT infrastructure.

(3) Ability to *survey and evaluate network usage, user complaints, traffic interruptions* or other communications *issues*, hardware and software *capabilities*, and other relevant factors.

(4) Ability to *plan, develop and implement security techniques, procedures, reporting requirements, and guidance* to ensure that *user access control* (physical, personnel, software, and information security) and other security requirements are in place.

In the next announcement, the keyword skills are also italicized. If you analyze the language of the vacancy announcements closely, you can find some interesting terms that you may never have seen in writing. I like the line about "finding, diagnosing, and eliminating human errors." It's true that supply technicians fix errors made by employees. This is not something you would write in your resume, unless you find it in a position description or vacancy announcement. But what a true statement! This term may not be a searchable term by the HR recruiter, but it certainly is a true statement for this job. Supply analysts should include this skill in their resume.

Announcement Analysis #2, Supply Technician, GS-7

Duties and responsibilities:

Inventory and Audit Branch Supply Management Division, Supply Department, Strategic Weapons Facility Atlantic (SWFLANT), Kings Bay, GA.

Technical supply department *inventory control program*, which includes

Physical count and audit functions, required to

Identify, isolate, and correct data system and *human errors*.

Planning, coordinating and *conducting physical inventories, audits*, and location surveys for assigned supply areas;

Analyzing stock records, material, and documentation to *diagnose and eliminate errors* and *initiating appropriate action*/coordination to prevent their recurrence;

Compiling inventory and audit data and preparing required periodic and special reports.

Plans, coordinates, and conducts all *physical inventories*, audits, and location survey for assigned supply areas.

Performs and coordinates *scheduled and unscheduled inventories* on spot, category, special, and location basis.

Inventories include a variety of units of issue i.e., set, assembly, square feet, cubic feet, pounds, etc.

Chapter Review

The importance of researching and analyzing vacancy announcements cannot be emphasized enough. You can use the text that is written in the duties and responsibilities sections to find the keywords for your resume, as well as give you ideas for writing your work experience section. This is valuable source material that can help you create an outstanding, on-target resume. Follow the systematic method of finding descriptive announcements, enlarging the type, and analyzing the content thoroughly. You will find wonderful phrases and descriptions that can change your resume. Why struggle to write descriptions of your jobs when the content is available to you with a little bit of research?

Chapter 7

One Resume Fits All

Make your career decisions before you write your resume.

The new automated system is more successful if you make important career decisions *before* writing your one electronic resume and submitting it to the database. All of the Job Kits described in Chapter 3 give instructions that you may submit only one resume at a time into each database. If you want to be considered for two or more job titles, then your resume must cover all job interests.

One Resume, Multiple Job Titles

Initially, the "one resume" concept caused concern for applicants because they couldn't believe or understand how one resume could cover more than one job. The former application system required hours of specific writing and tailoring of KSAs to fit each position. Now you write one resume that covers all of your specific career interests, submit it to the database, and update when you need to add new or changed information.

I have found in my resume-writing workshops that most people select job titles that are very much alike. Thereafter, when they make a list of their past job history, they can see on paper that the skills and qualifications easily cross over.

It is truly best to have one resume that is ready to submit for the various inventory building announcements. There are so many resume builders and resume databases that you have to have one resume ready to submit all the time! If you want to make changes to an existing resume, make the changes at least 48 hours before the closing date so that the resume will actually be in the database on the closing date. Many of the vacancy announcements for specific jobs are open only 5 days; this does not give you enough time to totally write your resume, only customize and submit!

You have to think about your strongest job skills before completing your resume. Most applicants are interested in one to four different jobs. The sample resumes on the CD-ROM have the job series written on the top of the resume. Here are a few of the combination resumes we have on the CD-ROM. If you look at the samples, you will see that the descriptions of jobs contain keywords and KSAs for each area of expertise.

Senior Scientist, Program Manager, Oceanographer

Management Analyst, Program Manager/Project Analyst, Computer Specialist

Administrative Officer, Program Operations Oversight, Supervisory Military Manpower Analyst

 Info The electronic resume samples on the CD-ROM demonstrate that one resume can work for multiple job interests.

Remember the types of positions you have applied for over the past year to18 months. Write down all of the job titles and series numbers. Here are a few examples:

* A **Writer-Editor** could also qualify as a **Visual Information Specialist.** The qualifications would be easy to fit for both series, and the duties and responsibilities would be similar.

* A **Material Handler** could also qualify as a **Logistics Specialist** with one resume. The qualifications would be similar and the duties and responsibilities would be similar as well. There could be some specialized skills or accomplishments that would be specific to each job, but that would not be difficult to cover both.

* A person who has been a **Computer Specialist** for the last five years and a **Management Analyst** with some computer responsibilities for the previous seven years would be a good combination for one resume. The qualifications would be easy to cover for both series, and the skills language would obviously be included within the description of each job.

* A **Financial Analyst, Accounting Specialist,** and **Budget Analyst** could easily be covered in one resume. The qualifica tions could be covered, and the skill language would be similar. The specific projects and skills should be reviewed and incorporated into the resume to make sure the software system finds the skill words for each industry.

Writing your "One Resume"

The correct approach to writing your One Resume is this:

1. Think about the job series for which you are qualified.

2. Find a vacancy announcement and position description for each. Look at the list of Web sites at the back of this book, so you can search for vacancy announcements.

3. Read the Qualifications section to see if you are qualified for the position.

4. Analyze these documents for language of the occupation.

5. Incorporate some of these words into your resume.

How do you know if you're qualified for a particular job?

In order to find out if you're qualified and to ensure that your resume will be successful with multiple occupational series searches, you need to review vacancy announcements or position descriptions for each of your selected job series. You can find these vacancy announcement Web sites in Chapter 3, "Job Kits Made Easier." More information on qualifying can be found in Chapter 5, "Getting Qualified."

Effective job combinations

At my workshops at USMC Materiel Command in Albany, Georgia, and Chief of Naval Education and Training in Pensacola, Florida, I asked the participants to list their job series interest. I wanted them to see that the One Resume concept is possible and realistic because the overall skills were usually compatible for their various job interests. Some said they would have to search vacancy announcements to find the correct job titles and see which positions match their skills. You will have to decide which occupational series you are seeking *before* you write and submit your electronic resume.

I have listed below approximately 30 job combinations named by participants from about 25 different workshops. Because of the missions of the two organizations — manufacturing, repair, and warehousing of military weapons in Albany, and education and training for all military services in Pensacola — the job titles include supply, logistics, administrative, computers, electronics, material handling, accounting, data management, training, and personnel.

Three job titles typically showed up together: Program Manager, Program Analyst, Management Analyst. These three positions involve similar managerial, analytical and special project skills in government. These jobs usually also involve writing, speaking, analyzing, report development, and special projects. The same person could write one resume for all three of these occupational series and be found qualified in a search.

Typical Government Job Combinations:

* Budget Analyst, Accounting Specialist, Financial Analyst

* Project Director, Management Specialist, Administrative Specialist

* Management Analyst, Program Analyst (and sometimes, Computer Specialist)

* Financial Operations Specialist, Budget Analyst, Systems Analyst

* Budget Analyst, Program Manager

* EEO Coordinator, Contract Specialist

* Program Manager, Program Analyst

* Secretary, Office Automation Assistant, Personnel Systems Administrator, EEO Assistant

* Secretary (OA), Computer Specialist, Administrative Assistant

* Data Clerk, Computer Assistant, Supply Clerk, Secretarial and Administrative

* Data Transcriber, Paralegal, Legal Secretary

* Data Transcriber, Computer Operator, Voucher Examiner

* Computer Specialist, Electrical Engineer

* Computer Specialist, Network Administrator, Webmaster, Programmer, Systems Administrator, Security

* Computer Assistant, Procurement (Information Technology), COTR, Contracts Specialist

* Computer Specialist, Program Analyst, Systems Analyst, Programmer, Equipment Analyst, Networking

* Logistics Data Management Assistant, Computer Specialist, Management Analyst

* Writer-Editor, Publication Specialist

* Technical Equipment Illustrator, Engineering Technician, Equipment Specialist

* Mechanical Engineer, Electrical Engineer

* Lead Firefighter, Automotive Mechanic, Electronics Technician

* Inventory Manager, Supply Systems Manager

* Supply Systems Analyst, Systems Analyst, Project Manager, Program Manager, Program Analyst

* Supply Technician, Inventory Management Specialist, Supply Systems Analyst

* Supply Technician, Project Manager, Inventory Manager

* Supply Systems Analyst, Cataloging, Inventory Manager

* Container Management Quality Control, Electronics (Combat Systems)

* QA Specialist, TMO Specialist, PP&P Specialist, Logistics, Supply

* Planner/Estimator, Inspector, Contractor/Surveillance

* Planner/Estimator, Warehouse Foreman, Inspector

* Freight Rate Specialist, Telecommunications Specialist, Transportation Specialist, Voucher Examiner

* Material Handler, Production Shop Planner, Inspector, Special Projects Section

* Material Handler, Receiving Specialist, Inventory Inspector

* Logistics Management Specialist (intern)

* Equipment Specialist, Quality Inspections

* Equipment Specialist, Inventory Manager, Quality Assurance Specialist, COTR

* Equipment Specialist, Quality Assurance, Logistics

Trying to Change Your Career?

There are two challenges to changing your career with the computer search system: You have to be qualified and you have to have the right words in your resume. In order to have the words in your resume, you have to gain experience in this new area through college courses, training, volunteer projects, task forces while on the job, committees, and job duties. These new skill words should be included in your resume so that a search for a particular set of skills zeroes in on yours.

Look on the Case Study section of the CD-ROM and Alan Cross' resumes and skills buckets. You will see that his first resume — the "before" resume — is unfocused and his skills bucket is broad. The "after" resume is more specific with nouns and technical terms for his areas of interest. The "after" resume and skills bucket contain much better terminology. His first resume was written for Writer-Editor and Public Affairs Specialist. The second one is more focused, targeted toward Career Transition, Human Resources, and Public Affairs. As a result of the revising his resume in this manner, Alan received five e-mails from human resources asking if he was interested in certain jobs.

Here are the two areas of consideration for a successful career change in an automated selection system.

1. **Personnel Rules:** A career change can be managed as long as you have the generalized and specialized experienced through paid or unpaid work experiences. Make sure you are qualified by reading the qualifications on the vacancy announcement. More on this in Chapter 5. If you are interested in an account-ing position and you have 24 credit hours in accounting, then you are basically qualified. If this announcement is written for the Outstanding Scholar Program, you need a GPA of 3.5 or over and you are qualified.

2. **Computer Search for Keywords:** The resume needs to include the skill words for a successful computer search. The account ing applicant will need to include accounting language through volunteer or part-time positions, accounting projects, account ing responsibilities in their current or previous positions. The accounting language needs to be there to be competitive with the search.

A Management Analyst may wish to move into a Career Transition counselor position. This person should have education, training or experience in counseling, leading a team, career transition counseling, organizational skills, meeting planning or other experiences which would contribute to career transition responsibilities. Some of the skills that were used as a Management Analyst will support a position as a Career Counselor (team work, analyzing information, producing reports, computer skills, interper-sonal skills).

A paralegal specialist can write a resume for a computer specialist job, if the paralegal specialist also performs computer chores and has returned to school for computer courses, such as a Networking Certificate or a certifica-tion in Information Systems.

Chapter Review

Write one resume that will cover multiple jobs.

You can have only one resume at one time in the database. If you submit an updated resume, the new resume will replace the old one.

Make sure that you read the Qualifications (generalized and specialized) on the announcement to determine if you are qualified for each job — more on this in the next chapter.

Read the duties and responsibilities to find keywords for your resume.

Ensure that your resume matches a particular search for a job.

Career changers have to make sure they have the qualifications for the new career and include the key words from the occupation for the computer skill search.

 **Tip** One resume is the best for today's electronic job search — whether you have your resume in an agency's database ready for unannounced searches or if you self-nominate for specific positions.

Time your resume updates carefully: It might take two to five days for your resume to actually "hit" the database after you update. If the job closes on a certain date, get your updates done ahead of time.

Part 4
Writing Your Resume

Chapter 8

Getting Started

"Getting started is the hardest part."

Writing a resume is a critical part of your career in private industry and now Federal government. If you're in the government, you're familiar with a long, detailed application form. Resume writing is new! So, let's analyze what it takes to really "get started" on your electronic resume.

Are You Motivated?

You have to be motivated to write this resuime. It seems difficult, but when you think about it, it's black and white. If you don't write this resume, you probably won't get promoted. If you want to be considered for positions with DOD agencies, you have to do your research. The end result of your effort will be referrals for more jobs and possibly even being offered positions with better money, better advancement opportunities, and more challenges and rewards.

1. Gather Your Materials

You need to gather written information about your work history. To demonstrate this very important part of preparing a resume, we will use a case study of an actual private industry job applicant. We're going to follow the processes he used to get ready to write his resume, such as finding specialized language, job titles, and jobs on DOD employment sites.

Meet John Green, an Electronics Locksmith at the University of Maryland in College Park, Maryland. An Electronics Locksmith is a highly skilled technician with expertise in both electronic and mechanical areas.

John is well organized and, consequently, has a three-ring binder filled with the following written documents that he will use to write his resume:

Position Descriptions (last four positions)

* Locksmith, Electronics, Building Security Unit, March 1999 to present

* Maintenance Structural Trade Chief II, Carpentry Shop, Physical Plant, 1988 to 1999

* Carpenter, 8/82 to 7/88

* Maintenance Mechanic Sr., 11/81 to 8/82

Performance Evaluations (last two positions)

* Letters from the University Chancellor, faculty, and administrators thanking him for his creative construction of displays and innovative carpentry

* Training certificates (numerous)

* Awards and recognitions for outstanding service in the Maintenance Department

Compiling your information

Compile any and all of the following information to begin writing your resume:

* SF-171, OF-621, Merit Promotion Application, Individual Development Plan

* Performance Evaluations

* Knowledge, Skills, and Abilities (KSAs) statements written in the recent past

* Resumes

* Training certifications and lists

* Awards and letters written from supervisors, team leaders, and customers

* Vacancy announcements from prior job searches

* Position Description for your current position and, if possible, for the positions you are seeking

2. Write an Outline of Your Job Titles

John is going to apply for positions using his experience and skills as a Carpenter, Electronics Locksmith, or Maintenance Mechanic. The position titles will be different in DOD agencies, but he knows he has valuable skills that can be used at military bases. Here is his career history with job titles and dates:

University of Maryland, College Park, in the Physical Plant
for 15 years.

> Locksmith, Electronics, Building Security Unit, 3/99 to present
>
> Maintenance Structural Trade Chief II, Carpentry Shop,
> Physical Plant, 7/88 to 3/99
>
> Carpenter, 8/82 to 7/88
>
> Maintenance Mechanic Sr., 11/81 to 8/82
>
> Maintenance Mechanic, 9/80 to 11/81
>
> Maintenance Service Worker II, 5/80 to 9/80
>
> Maintenance Service Worker I, 11/79 to 5/80
>
> Carpenter's Helper, 5/79 to 11/79

U.S. Army, 1975–1979, Honorably Discharged

John's final electronic resume includes jobs back to 1980 — 20 years of
experience. Most resumes emphasize the last 10 years and then summarize
early experience.

3. Update Your Project List

John read over his current position description (PD) and realized that his
recent projects were not included in the PD. His current job title was still
Maintenance Chief, which didn't reflect his job duties. He was performing the
job of an Electronics Locksmith. When he did his research, he searched for
jobs that reflected the duties he performed, not the specific job title.

Here's a list of recent projects that were not included in the generic position
descriptions. These projects written as nouns (proper names and titles) could
be important in his resume.

Locksmith, Electronics, Building Security Unit,
March 1999 to present

PROJECTS:

* Installed the Protag system on more than 200 computers in the McKeldin Library — Required installation with DSC panel alarms.

* Access Control — Replaced old Northern system with Nextel.

* Installed Level Access control.

* Programming — Wiring for the MC25 Program involving installation of specialized wiring for delayed relays for handicapped door opening systems.

* Installed more than 200 automatic door openers.

* Photo Beam — Installed the first photo beam system in the McKeldin Library that was tied to alarm panel.

Maintenance Structural Trade Chief II, Carpentry Shop, Physical Plant, 1988 to 1999

PROJECTS:

* Northern Access Control replacements — Installations.

* Lock Standalone systems — V-serial.

* Installed access controls for handicap access. Resolved an access problem for handicapped operations when a student was unable to open the door after hours. Designed and in stalled a delayed relay wiring system to enable access to door opening systems after hours.

* Converted key lock to card lock system, setting up record-keeping system, and updating codes.

* Overhead Doors — Shop expert on overhead door installations and troubleshooting.

4. Researching Agency Web Sites

Because John is planning to apply to a DOD agency, he is going to search the Army, Air Force, and Navy Web sites. John is searching these Web sites for three reasons:

1. For vacancy announcements that will contain skill language for carpenter, locksmith, electronics, and/or maintenance mechanic positions

2. For the equivalent DOD job titles

3. For positions that he could apply for when the resume is completed

www.cpol.army.mil

John has decided to begin his research with the Army's Web site for the National Capital Region and goes first to the Army's Employment Web site.

Next, John clicks on Jobs → Army's Vacancy Announcements → Career Program Positions. This link says: Normally GS-13s, 14s, 15s. John will not be a GS-13, 14, or 15, but his search does not fit any of the other links offered. John was able to search for Carpenter through the list of all the jobs. He found an announcement with a good description of his skills.

The vacancy announcement that John found for Carpenter, WG-4607, Grade 9 has some great keywords for the carpenter position:

> Performs journeyman level carpentry tasks to construct, alter, repair, and modify buildings and structures, fittings, panels, partitions, and other wood or wood substitute components. Perform painting, sheet metal, plumbing, electrical tasks such as moving an electric box when putting in sheetrock, that are incidental to carpentry tasks. Other carpentry tasks includes planning and laying out work in accordance with drawings, sketches, blueprints, and own knowledge of construction or needed repairs. Selects lumber, materials and other supplies. Responsible for measuring and filling in gaps on incomplete blueprints, sketches and work orders. Installs rafters, studs, sills, plate braces, joists, floors, sub-floors, panels (to include sheetrock, plywood and veneers), siding sheeting, roofing, building paper, insulating materials, door and window frames, and interior and exterior trim. Installs or repairs floor, wall or coiling tile, including dropped-ceilings. This includes such tasks as glazing, the installation of locksets, roof repairs, screening countertops, cabinets, and paneling. Plumbing and electrical, during carpentry work that might involve modifying fixtures, fittings, pumps, etc., and electrical tasks such as rearranging old or installing new outlets, light fixtures in existing systems or moving electrical outlet when moving or rearranging or sheetrock are performed in connection with carpenter work.

This announcement also included knowledge, skills, and abilities for the carpenter position. This is excellent for John's resume — all of these skills are John's!

Knowledge, Skills, and Abilities (KSAs):

1. Ability to do the work of the carpenter without more than normal supervision. (Screen-out element, or required element)

2. Technical practices (theoretical, precise, artistic)

3. Ability to interpret instructions, specifications, etc. (includes blueprint reading)

4. Ability to use and maintain tools and equipment

5. Knowledge of materials

http://www.afpc.randolph.af.mil/resweb

John is feeling optimistic, so he goes to the Air Force Web site to see if there are any positions for Carpenter or Electronics Technician positions.

There are hundreds of job listings, but none for Carpenters. He sees a job title, Electronic Equipment Specialist, and recognizes that this job represents a lot of the skills he has. In government job searches, you have to fit your experience into Uncle Sam's job titles. This announcement also has a great description for "Specialized Individual Occupational Requirements." You never know what you're going to find in Federal job announcements. They are all different and you'll have to read them. There are some excellent keywords and skills in this description. This description is converted into a Skills List that is listed at the end of this chapter.

Electronic Equipment Specialist

Major Duties: This is a series in which the Air Force might have opportunities. Electronics Technician GS-0856 - Electronics technicians apply a knowledge and understanding of electronic subject matter in performing work connected with the development and evaluation of design characteristics of all kinds of equipment, devices, and systems that embody electronic principles. They test and operate such equipment in order to establish its operating characteristic parameters, and permissible tolerances. Specialized Individual Occupational Requirements: Specialized Experience (for positions at GS-4 and above): Examples of qualifying specialized experience include: 1. Work as technician, instructor, inspector, or mechanic (civilian or military) that shows progression in theoretical and practical knowledge of electronic theory, and of the characteristics, function, operation, and capabilities of a variety of types of electronic equipment. This experience must have included the use of schematic diagrams, a variety of test equipment, and the application of appropriate electronic formulas involved in such duties as testing, troubleshooting, modifying, designing, calibrating, installing, maintaining, repairing, constructing, developing, and instructing on electronic equipment, or similar functions. 2. Experience in developing policies, standards, and procedures for maintenance, installation, or similar functions, provided the work clearly shows that the applicant applied a specialized knowledge of the theories and principles of a variety of electronic systems or equipment. 3. Experience doing bench repair of television and radio receivers in a commercial shop in which the applicant does troubleshooting on a variety of equipment, and uses such special test equipment as sweep generators, marker generators, oscilloscopes, and other equipment normally employed in such servicing. This opening will be acceptable as specialized experience at GS-6 and below, if applicable to the work of the position.

John is having great success in finding positions that provide him with the DOD language. John has already found two titles that were acceptable for his qualifications: Carpenter (Army) and Electronic Equipment Specialist (AF).

www.donhr.navy.mil

John decides to go to the Navy's Web site to see what kind of jobs, job titles, and descriptions he can find for his resume. The Navy's Web site has U.S. Marines civilian military jobs also.

John clicks on Job Opportunities → Searchable Job Opportunity Database → Search on All Open Positions. He clicks on POSITION TITLE to alphabetize the job title list.

John does not find the job titles Carpenter and Electronic Equipment Specialist, but he does find Woodcrafter Leader. John is a team leader in his job, so this job will fit his experience. He copies and pastes the text from the duties and responsibilities text into a word processing file so that he can study the language.

Woodcrafter Leader

Coordinates work while assuring proper inter-trade and inter-shop coordination, high levels of quality assurance with timely yet orderly job completion. Demonstrates proper work methods. Provides on-the-job training for workers under his/her leadership, corrects improper wood crafter work methods, ensures assigned work procedures, such as TGI's, process instructions and work-related shipyard instructions and processes are being followed. Answers questions of the supervisor on overall work operations and problems. Ensures safe work practices and good housekeeping while assuring timely tool, equipment, material, and procedure availability. Keeps the first line supervisor informed of job progress, as well as technical, personnel, material, equipment needs and job performance. Must be able to perform, without close supervision, journeyman level wood crafter work.

Research Results

Success! John used the three civilian agency Web sites to find three announcements and job titles that will fit his experience! Some of this language will be incorporated into his electronic resume. John is going to write a "one resume fits all" resume so that he can "play the game" by submitting his resume to all of the databases for jobs for which he seems qualified.

Past titles from University of Maryland:

* Locksmith, Electronics

* Maintenance Structural Trade Chief II, Carpentry Shop, Physical Plant

Equivalent DOD job titles:

* Carpenter, WG-4607, Grade 9 (Army)

* Electronics Technician GS-0856 (Air Force)

* Woodcrafter Leader (Navy)

 Info John Green's electronic One Resume was written for three job series: Carpenter, Woodcrafter Leader, and Electronics Technician. See John's resume in the Appendix of this book and on the CD-ROM.

Chapter Review

Take the time to get ready to write your resume by gathering past employment materials, updating your project list, and researching Web sites for job titles, keywords and descriptions, and job opportunities. After you've finished this preparation work, you can start to write!

 Info MOTIVATION: The end result of your research will be an outstanding resume that will get results!

 Info Internet Search for Industry Language: Search for vacancy announcements with current descriptions and key words. Sometimes "Duties and Responsibilities" in the vacancy announcements are short and generic. If you find generic ones, keep looking for another announcement.

Web Site Research Sources

Army's National Capital Region:

http://www.cpol.army.mil/

Air Force:

http://www.afpc.randolph.af.mil/resweb

Navy:

http://www.donhr.navy.mil

Dictionary of Occupational Titles:

http://www.oalj.dol.gov/libdot.htm

Info The skills listed in this chapter and on the CD-ROM are just a sample of skills. Every manager's position description of each job is going to be different, therefore different skills will be extracted. A skill is a skill is a skill — if you explain that you've done it and the same skills are in a position description, there will be a match when there is a search for qualified candidates.

Electronic Equipment Specialist Skills List of Keywords

Blueprint	Carpentry Experience
Construction Work	Drop Ceilings
Electrical Hardware	Electricity
Exterior Trim	Exteriors
Facilities Changes	Facilities Maintenance
Filling Orders	Floor Installation
Floor Repair	Glazing
Insulating Material	Interior Trim
Material Selection	Metals
Painting	Patching
Plumbing	Pumps
Remodeling	Roofing
Sheet Metal	Sheetrock
Sketching	Structural Repair
Tile	Work Measurement
Work Order	Underlayment

Chapter 9

Work Experience

*Ninety percent of your resume is
your work experience.*

The most difficult — yet most important — part of your resume is the work experience section. This chapter includes six mini-chapters that will inspire you to write an outstanding work experience section.

A. Intoduction to Work Experience (pg 123)

B. Creating an outline with your "hats, nouns, and skills" (pg 133)

C. Filling in your outline with your duties and responsibilities (pg 146)

D. What have you accomplished lately? (pg 152)

E. What happened to your KSAs? (pg158)

F. Putting it all together (pg 167)

A. INTRODUCTION TO WORK EXPERIENCE

In with the New, Out with the Old

Writing about what you do at work isn't easy. Federal jobs are complex to describe because of the largeness of government and the various branches, offices, components, units, contractors, customers, and types of work. This chapter is going to help you think clearly about your job so that you can write it a new way — in plain English.

The new writing style is more direct and includes more details. Compare the two styles for yourself.

The Old Bureaucratic Writing Style vs. The New Resume Style of Writing

Old:

Manpower Analyst assigned to Assessment Team to support Navy Manpower Analyst Center tasking under the NMRS Contract. Performed Navy manpower requirements determination, mobilization resource analysis and

---

Efficiency Review application studies for designated activity groups. Analyzed report authorization and manyear equivalents for selected activities. Served as an analyst for the study and development of various documents. Responsible for the collection and analyzing of data necessary to produce those documents required. Other duties consisted of briefings to various management levels. This effort included a thorough analysis of the functions of thirteen existing manpower systems that have been identified, as well as studying numerous interfaces with other Navy Information Systems.

New:

Manpower Analyst and Member of an Assessment Team within the Navy Manpower Analyst Center. Analyzed Navy manpower requirements, mobilization resources and manyear equivalents to produce Efficiency Studies. Analyzed 13 activity groups, including: logistics, contracts, finances, training and project management and their working relationships with Navy Information Systems. Interviewed managers, collected, organized and analyzed data; created Excel spreadsheets; and wrote and edited more than 250 pages presented to senior management. RESULTS: Discovered the need for establishing benchmarks and performance measures to improve the accuracy of efficiency information within all 13 units. Recommended increased funding to budget officers based on existing manpower, needed resources and the growth of military activities in the year 2001.

What's the Difference?

The first version is true, but it is bureaucratic, boring, and unclear. The paragraph says what this person is *responsible for* — not what the person *did*. Note the number of passive — rather than active — phrases. There are a lot of wasted words and the specifics of the project are not included. This person is studying efficiency for a reason, but the results are not here.

The second description is interesting and valuable to the organization. This person is studying the efficiency and utilization of resources for 13 divisions. This is important research for accurate budgeting for future missions. The individual's skills are clear:

Research	Analysis
Investigation	Interviewing
Data Compilation	Writing
Editing	Spreadsheet Development
Making Recommendations	Presentations

The results of the research are included, along with more details of the project. Much better. I'm impressed.

Now this person sounds like an excellent management analyst — a gifted candidate with multiple skills and the ability to achieve results! (Not to mention the ability to write a resume that makes an excellent impression.) A thorough, well-written resume speaks highly of a person, announcing to the hiring manager that this candidate is thorough, precise, and dynamic in presenting him or herself.

Why is it so hard to write a clear, understandable description of your jobs?

The problems with writing a clear, easy-to-understand work experience description are many. From the many resume-writing workshops I have led, here are some of the reasons why Federal employees have difficulty writing about their jobs.

Many Federal employees:

* Have been writing their SF-171s in the bureaucratic style cited above.

* Have depended on their SF-171s and PDs as a basis of job information. Because of the massive changes in government in the last eight years, most PDs are out-of-date, which leaves them without an up-to-date outline of their duties.

* Have not updated their SF-171s within the last year — or perhaps in the last 15 years.

* Can't remember everything they do in their jobs because they do so much.

* Don't recognize or think about what is most important in their work.

* Don't realize the value they bring to their offices, co-workers, supervisors, and customers.

* Aren't appreciated for their efforts in many cases.

* Don't get enough feedback from supervisors.

* Don't understand their role in the "big picture" or the mission of the organization.

* Don't know the difference between a responsibility and an accomplishment.

* Don't talk about their jobs enough.

* Don't get excited or passionate about their work.

* Do the work of several employees due to reorganization and haven't kept track of what they are actually doing.

* Don't keep a list of accomplishments, so they forget.

* Are bored and under-challenged, so they don't think about what they're doing.

* Perform routinely, so they don't know what they're doing.

It's time to clarify these inaccurate job titles, unclear duties, and unrewarded outstanding efforts. Employee-supervisor communication is going to get better, but even if it doesn't, you can do more to gain information and awareness of your job and your role so that you can write an outstanding resume that sells your skills and accomplishments.

Resume Writing Is Self-Promotion

Marketing and selling yourself is a new concept to Federal employees. The word "selling" is foreign to Federal employees, but when you're looking for a new job or promotion, you are selling yourself! And nowadays, your number one marketing tool is your resume. There will be new position descriptions, new incentives, new mission statements, and more reorganization (probably), as well as a renewed effort to keep the highest-quality employees. It's going to be up to you to sell yourself to this new government.

There is a "likeability factor" with resumes. To become the best-qualified person for the job, it's helpful if you seem likeable to the selecting official. Even though this is an electronic resume, the paper version will be read by the selecting official. Your resume needs to stand out when the selecting official has the top 15 resumes on his desk.

A resume is a marketing piece that presents the positive. You need to impress the reader that you are a quality, high-performing, skilled, efficient, knowledgeable, and hard-working employee. You are selling yourself to two audiences:

Info

What is the Likeability Factor in a resume? It is how interesting you are to the reader from reading the resume. If there is something unique about your resume that makes the resume stand out, and make you seem likeable, then you have a high likeability factor in your resume. Ask yourself these questions: Is your resume interesting? Is there something unique about your background? What stands out? Do you appear to be service-driven and team-oriented? A resume can be either interesting or routine. Make your resume interesting with special projects, community service, and interpersonal skills.

In one of my workshops we were discussing likeability factors and accomplishments. Here's a few interesting accomplishments these employees will add to their resumes: An audiovisual specialist remembered that his production team won the equivalent to an "Emmy" for a Navy Seals video! An education specialist remembered he did a five-week research project in Washington, D.C. and realized from the pleased audience what an accomplishment that was! Another education specialist remembered that the Navy Band Conductor appreciated all the effort she went through to help him finish his B.S. degree! These are interesting facts that make these employees likeable.

* The artificial intelligence in the software (for the initial searching)

* The hiring manager who will receive your paper resume

That hiring manger will receive resumes from 10 to 15 candidates who are supposedly equally qualified. If your resume stands out, you will receive a phone call for further consideration. If you can interview well on the phone or in person, you could get the job.

Recognizing your skills, the variety of your responsibilities, challenges you've met, and your accomplishments is more important now with the new resume.

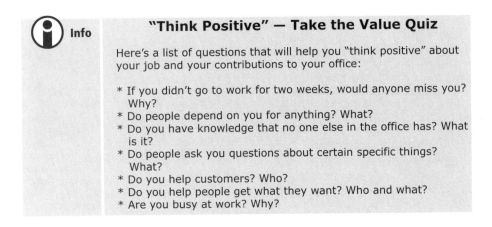

Info

"Think Positive" — Take the Value Quiz

Here's a list of questions that will help you "think positive" about your job and your contributions to your office:

* If you didn't go to work for two weeks, would anyone miss you? Why?
* Do people depend on you for anything? What?
* Do you have knowledge that no one else in the office has? What is it?
* Do people ask you questions about certain specific things? What?
* Do you help customers? Who?
* Do you help people get what they want? Who and what?
* Are you busy at work? Why?

When you write the answers to these questions, you will have information that you can use in your resume. The answers to these questions can help you recognize what you do, for whom, how busy you are, what expertise you have, and how valuable you are to your office. If you are not busy and no one would miss you except your friends, then you really need to change jobs.

Frequently Asked Questions about Work Experience

Here are some important frequently asked questions from my workshop participants about the work experience section.

How important is my current job compared to the previous positions?

* Your most recent position is your most important. The most recent position is where the hiring managers will be focusing their attention.

* If a previous position were really your most important position, then you should feature that position, rather than the current job.

* 90% of the knowledge, skills, and abilities will come from the work experience section.

* Your current job write-up could be three paragraphs to a page in length.

* You could spend two hours or more on writing your current work experience alone.

* You should write an outline for your current position. (See the *Hats, Nouns, and Verbs* section)

What if my position description doesn't reflect what I really do? Should I write about what I do or follow the position description?

* Many position descriptions are out-of-date because of the fast-changing organizations.

* You should read your PD and use what you can — if anything. Then you should write about what you really do in your job.

* You will have to find vacancy announcements that will include more current PD language that can help you write about your job responsibilities.

My job title has changed and it doesn't really mean anything. What can I do about that? I don't really do the work of my job title. Will it affect the way the computer scans my resume?

* You should use your current title in the description of the job details. But when you describe your duties, write about what you really do. This is a typical format for Federal jobs because many job titles are inaccurate — especially Program Analyst, Management Analyst. More realistic (however unofficial) titles for these jobs might be: Analyst,Writer-Editor, Special Projects Coordinator, Researcher, Facilitator.

Should I use my SF-171 descriptions for the work experience?

* If you copy and paste your SF-171 text into the resume, the descriptions may not be in the plain language. Your resume skills bucket may not have the right words because the old bureaucratic writing style is not the same as today's plain language writing style. Your resume needs to match the job announcement language.

* If you held a job prior to your current position which is significant and supports your job objectives, then describe this job in detail as well.

How far back should I go?

* There is no rule about how far back to go with your dates and jobs. The SF-171 gave instructions to include 10 years. You can go back further if you like, but synopsize earlier experiences.

* The last five to ten years experience are the most important and relevant for your job search.

* Rather than focus on chronology, write about your most relevant positions.

How many jobs should be included?

* Combine jobs which were really the same job, but with different grade levels, different locations, different names of organizations. If the job is the same, describe it in one job block.

* If your organization was disestablished a few years ago and the organization name and your job title changed, you could still write this as one job because your job did not change-only the organization. You held the same job during reorganization.

* If you were downsized and you now have a job that is one grade lower than the previous job, but is the same job series, you should write about both grade levels in separate job blocks. Focus on the higher level, but consider if you will be able to return to the higher level. If not, focus the resume where you are now.

* Analyze the number of jobs you have held and decide which positions you will list on your electronic resume. Most people list three to four jobs. Most resume builders have space for up to six job listings.

* Do not worry about covering all of the dates in your career. However, the new electronic resume should include most recent and relevant jobs.

Should a part-time business, volunteer work, service in the reserves, and a variety of military positions be considered a "job"?

* If you have a significant volunteer job, you can write this experience as though it were a paid job. The resume includes both paid and unpaid experience.

* If you have a part-time business, you can list this as a separate job. If you are trying to change careers and your small business provides skills that will support your career change, describe your business in detail. Remember the software will only find the skills that you write in your resume.

* If you are in the reserves, you should list the reserves as a job with dates of service, description, and supervisor(s).

* If you were in the military and held numerous positions, you can highlight the last one or two jobs and then summarize experience prior to that.

* If you were in the military years ago, you can summarize all of your military experience into one job block.

Should you cover every minute of your job history?

* If you left government and took a position that is not relevant to your current career, you can leave it out. Again, the key is *relevant* job listings.

* The SF-171 required that you fill in every period of time in your career — even if you stayed at home, took care of a family member, traveled, went to school, or got well from an accident. The new resume should include relevant experience only. (There's that word *relevant* again!)

* Perhaps your most recent position is not the most relevant for your current objective. If so, you should emphasize the most significant positions. The software will read your entire resume; it doesn't matter whether your most relevant position appears first or second.

* Remember that the resume is read by the computer for skills and keyword phrases. Also remember that a hiring manager will actually see your resume and read it. It's important to make your resume readable and interesting.

What You'll Need to Get Started

Here's a list of what you need to start writing your new resume:

* Training lists
* SF-171, SF-612, resume
* Military info/DD214
* Position Descriptions
* Previous vacancy announcements
* Performance evaluations
* Program descriptions and/or product description
* Service descriptions
* Awards and letters of commendation
* Paid and unpaid work experience
* List of accomplishments
* SF-50 (for dates and salary information)

Step 1. Begin writing your resume. Use the samples on the CD-ROM now!

The steps to writing your electronic resume using the samples on the CD-ROM are as follows:

1. Open the CD-ROM.

2. Open the Electronic Resume Samples.

3. Find a sample that is close to your job title and grade.

4. Open the resume sample.

5. Save it on your hard drive with a new name.

6. Use "replace text" to make this resume yours. In other words, replace that person's information with yours.

You will see the job description information for the sample person. You need to replace the first job experience with your information.

Start replacing text with the first job.

Below is the text from an Administrative Officer, GS-12. Type your information in the file instead of this text. After you type in your information, delete the sample material.

JOHN WALTON BASKINS

SSN: 000000000

324 E. Encore Dr.

Hanford, CA 93230

Home Phone: 555 900-1111

Work Phone: 555 900-2999

Email Address: jwbaskins@aol.com

WORK EXPERIENCE

08/1996 to present; 40 hours per week; **ADMINISTRATIVE OFFICER**, GS-0341-12; $65,000 annually. Naval Air Station, 700 Avenger Ave., Lemoore, CA 93246; Supervisor, CDR Tim Brown, 555 999-3333, permission to contact, and LCDR John Smith, Director of Administration, Navy Region Southwest, 937 North Harbor Drive, San Diego, CA 92132-0058, 999 555-0002, permission to contact.

B. HATS, NOUNS, AND SKILLS

How many "hats" do you wear at work?

You wear multiple "hats" in your job! You may be a team leader, supervisor, contract manager, administrator, database manager, and network manager. Or you might be a management assistant, office manager, computer support person, scheduler, meeting planner, researcher, and problem-solver. Each of these job titles represents a "hat" you wear.

Reading that bureaucratic paragraph in the previous chapter should inspire you to want to write a totally new draft of your work experience. The best way to write about your job is to create an outline using nouns, or verbs, to define your job responsibilities. Using more nouns will increase your success with database searches and improve your resume's readability by your human readers. Nouns are easy to understand and have known meanings.

Step 2. Create your work experience outline with nouns or verbs

1. Look at the sample outlines in this chapter.

2. Create an outline for your current or most important recent position.

3. Use nouns or verbs to categorize each functional area.

4. Type your outline on the disk just like you see here in the example.

5. Replace the text that is on the disk.

> **WORK EXPERIENCE**
>
> 08/1996 to present; 40 hours per week; **ADMINISTRATIVE OFFICER**, GS-0341-12; $65,000 annually. Naval Air Station, 700 Avenger Ave., Lemoore, CA 93246; Supervisor, CDR Tim Brown, 555 999-3333, permission to contact, and LCDR John Smith, Director of Administration, Navy Region Southwest, 937 North Harbor Drive, San Diego, CA 92132-0058, 999 555-0002, permission to contact.
>
> ADMINISTRATION FOR THE NAVAL AIR STATION:
>
> SUPPORT SERVICES:
>
> PROGRAM OPERATIONS OVERSIGHT:
>
> BUDGET FORMULATION AND EXECUTION:
>
> INTERNAL SECURITY:
>
> OFFICIAL MAIL CENTER:
>
> EMPLOYEE TRAINING:
>
> TRAVEL MANAGEMENT:
>
> MANPOWER MANAGEMENT:
>
> PERSONNEL, HUMAN RESOURCES:

Create a Work Experience Outline

Remember when you were in school and you had a major paper to write? The teacher asked you to come up with a topic and create an outline. That's what you are doing with your Work Experience Outline. After you have an outline, you fill in the descriptions of your responsibilities, skills, and knowledge.

The "Hats and Nouns" exercise is a favorite in my workshops. My participants easily recite the "hats" they wear and learn quickly what I mean by creating an outline with nouns or skills. This exercise results in a clear outline of the activities they actually do at work and the roles they play, thus resulting in organized and logical descriptions.

Here are several examples from my workshops to get you started writing your outline. A few of the outlines contain a short description of a particular area of work.

After you develop your outline, you will probably consolidate certain areas of work into one. For instance, you might combine team leader and project manager. Or you might combine researcher, analyst, editor and writer. You can typically discover that you have three to eight major roles you play.

Remember you are compiling an outline that will lead to a new and interesting job write-up. Try and find any of your "hats" or roles for your job outline.

Program Manager

Sole management analyst for civilians for the Director of Information Systems Services Department

Team leader/facilitator for Information Technology

Systems manager

Computer operator and database administrator (or monitor, manager)

Project manager/coordinator

Assistant contracting officer representative

Consultant or technical advisor

Visual Information Specialist

Illustrator — visual aids for classrooms for Navy Schools

Briefs — design

Graphics designer using CorelDraw

Posters and booklets

Client consultant — conceptualize, plan, visualize, and structure graphics needed to meet the needs of customers

Project coordinator and team member

Acting supervisor

Trainer

Management Analyst

Lead software tester and troubleshooter

Web site consultation and updates; content administrator

Researcher — develop queries in Oracle

Researcher — acquisition requirements

Project coordinator

Budget coordinator / resource requirements management and tracking

Analyst/problem-solver

Monitor and test system performance — create solutions for customers

Customer service and client coordination

Writer/ editor of correspondence and documentation

Briefings preparation

Meeting chair

Team member

Trainer

Administrative Librarian

Library coordinator

Manager

Inventory control/Researcher

Trainer and educator

Patron services manager

Workshop designer and leader

Program policy developer and interpretation

Client consultation and customer services — review services, problem-solving, consultation, and improvement of library services

Internet and online database search

Multimedia manager — Web scanning technology

Writer-editor of public information and marketing materials

Education Technician

Acting Assistant Director
Test control officer
Test scheduler
Administrator
Customer service representative
Counselor
Briefings and presentations
Trainer
Supervisor

Military Personnel Clerk

Travel coordinator/consultant — TAD
Collect, review, forward for payment
Travel orders per week (example: 20 to 40 domestic and abroad)
Travel agency liaison
Permanent change of station orders
Advance pay
Authorized Visa IMPAC holder
Knowledge of policies and procedures
Personnel files management
Writer and editor of correspondence
Classified message board and correspondence management
Problem solving
Customer services/liaison/public relations

Financial Programs Analyst

Payroll technician
Analyst
Credit card and travel card analyst
Researcher and problem-solver

Administrative Clerk

Researcher, statistical technician

Computer technician

Communications customer liaison

Secretary

Administrative, computer and public relations support for entire division of five professionals, operations division director, chief, and others

Computer operations and database updates in Excel

Publications assistant

Historical research and assistance

Internet research

Schedule meetings and visitors; research documentation

Proofreader and editor

Writer and composer of letters, correspondence, and reports

Public relations and customer services

Daily morning reports production

Maintain chronological history

File management

Appointment and schedule management

Document management — scan and upload/download to/from Internet

Software: WordPerfect, Lotus Suite, MS Word and Office Suite, PowerPoint

Team Leader and Supervisor

Liaison with other DOD agencies on equipment matters, meetings

Technical assistance, preparing briefs, consultants, testing of new equipment

Command liaison on newly fielded items

Liaison command corrosion control

ISO 9000 lead auditor

QA specialist

Audits and inspections

Technical advisor and assistance

Technical manual reviews

Maintenance management

Production control

Calibration review

Troubleshooting

Contract review

Contractor liaison

Contractor process review (example: review contract performance on six-month basis; evaluate and give written statement on performance of contractors)

Statement of work (example: review and revise recommendations)

Work scheduler — set work standards

Writer (example: fitness reports and evaluations; work procedures and processes)

Trainer and instructor

Transportation supervisor

Supervisory Mechanical-Electrical Engineer

Counselor and supervisor

Engineer and designer

Cost-estimator

Specification writer

Evaluator/reviewer

Interviewer

Team leader

Project coordinator

Problem-solver

Supply Technician

Customer service liaison and technical resource

Technical assistant — managing supply systems

Researcher

Database technician

Problem-solver

Stratification and purchasing

Supply Systems Analyst

Management analyst

Configuration management specification, maintenance

Researcher

Systems installation

Database management

Supply Systems Analyst

Data systems analyst

Cataloguing system

Weapon program manager — transitions and reconciliations

Problem-solver — error research and incident reports investigation

Tester

Writer — system maintenance requests

Communications

Customer Services

Quality Assurance Specialist

Computer system

Statistical analysis (example: extracting data, statistical techniques, develop curriculum, methods and systems for improving utilization of the system by users)

Quality control

ISO auditor and team member (example: perform corrective and preventive analysis)

Coordinator/customer liaison (example: customers: contractors and Marine Corps fleet)

Analyst (example: output from contractors)

Problem-solver

User support

Writer of results from contractor utilization and evaluations

Trainer

Telecommunications Specialist

Computer specialist

Project assistant (example: Manage an average of 4 ongoing projects, with specific timelines and customer interface. Utilize Microsoft software to project benchmarks and meet deadlines.)

Technical advisor

Evaluator

Cost analyzer

Team leader

Configuration Data Management Specialist

Project manager (example: manage three projects...)

Tester

Evaluator

Communications and customer liaison

Board chair (secretariat)

Track configuration status accounts

Configuration manager

Database maintenance

WG3 Labor

(Also qualified for: Aircraft Machinist, Motor Vehicle Operator, Landscape Specialist)

Installation logistics — grounds and structures

Landscaping

Grounds maintenance

Plumbing

Electrical

Sewage and storm drains

Special events logistics and coordination

Hazardous material handler

Respirator qualified

Safety training

Third vice president — union representative

Union representative, A 76 team

Chair, arbitration panel

Union steward, Maintenance Branch

Clothing Designer

Trainer

Design engineer, computer aided design (CAD)

Project manager

Quality assurance manager

Consultant

Customer service liaison

Equipment Specialist/Quality Assurance Specialist

Validator and screening

Equipment sampling, research, testing

Auditor

Investigator

Inspector/quality assurance (list equipment)

Writer-editor — instructional materials (example: review and write changes)

Database maintenance

Customers (example: list names of customers, i.e. clothing sales stores for Marine Corps worldwide; textiles, tents, 782 gear)

Statement of work/contract monitoring

Customer liaison/Communication

Technical advisory

Team assistance member

Equipment Specialist/ Supervisor

Program manager

Inventory manager

Logistics coordination

Resource management

ISO program manager

Supervisor and team leader

EEO Counselor

Committee member

Problem-solver

Customer liaison — internal and external

Trainer

Contract manager

Scheduler

Electric Motor Mechanic

Equipment installer: AAV, CNG, compression natural gas

Analyze and test

Troubleshooter

Fabricator

Customer services

Electronic Technician

Lead technician

Research and data collection

Troubleshooter and calibration expert

Parts management and inventory control

Repairing and installation

Quality assurance

Customer service and consultation

Surveyor

Trainer

Team member

Safety

Equipment and skills list

Industrial Waste Treatment Plant Operator

Operations and maintenance

Maintenance technician

Hazardous waste technician

Potable water technician

Supervisory Oceanographer and Physical Scientist

Supervisor and team leader (examples: staff, training, evaluations, discipline, EEO, delegation of duties, skills analysis, position description, mentoring, meeting planning)

Manager (examples of areas of management: budget, purchasing, negotiation)

Project manager (examples of elements of project management: plan timelines, schedule, resources, assignment, skill analysis, troubleshooting, research)

Subject matter expert and consultant

Agency liaison with R&D agency, fleet, Navy

Research coordinator or data collector

Problem solver

Writer-editor

Trainer

Traffic Management Officer

Interpreter of regulations and entitlements for customers

Supervisor

Budget manager

COR (example: manage and evaluate contractor performance)

Passport agent

Office administration

Writer

Secretary — Administrative

Information management (information managed: correspondence; reports, database entries, personnel forms)

Computer skills / proficiencies — MS Word, Excel, Access,

PowerPoint, Corel WordPerfect Suite, Internet, e-mail

Communications — interpersonal skills

Customer relations with personnel, senior management, teams, task forces

Writing/editing

Administration (types of administrative skills: streamlining, organizing, planning, efficiency systems)

Timekeeping and payroll (sample language: manage records for 140 employees, including communicating with employees regarding benefits, time and changing employee information)

Scheduling meetings/conferences

Purchasing, contracting, procurement, working vendors

Training — conducting training and coordinating scheduling of training for employees

Travel — arranging itineraries, agenda planning

Support senior management and engineers in special projects.

Clerical, administrative, filing, phones, mail

What's Next?

Did you recognize yourself in any of the lists above? The next section will help you "Fill in Your Outline" with the descriptions of your duties either taken from your past written materials or from your memory of what you do at work.

Section Review

In order to write a new draft of your current or most recent work experience, create an outline of the "hats" you wear at work. These are your major roles or jobs. Use as many nouns as you can. Nouns are descriptive, searchable, and readable by hiring managers and computers.

 Info Don't depend on your 171, 612, or PD to come up with what you really do at work! The "old style" of writing may not include all of the roles you play at work.

C. FILLING IN YOUR OUTLINE

Selling yourself begins now. Filling in the outline with skills, experiences, accomplishments, and the magic words looks simple, but this is the "meat" of the resume. Get ready.

In my resume writing workshops, participants struggle with writing the work experience section more than any other section.

Step 3. Fill in your work experience outline

WORK EXPERIENCE

08/1996 to present; 40 hours per week; ADMINISTRATIVE OFFICER, GS-0341-12; $65,000 annually. Naval Air Station, 700 Avenger Ave., Lemoore, CA 93246; Supervisor, CDR Tim Brown, 555 999-3333, permission to contact, and LCDR John Smith, Director of Administration, Navy Region Southwest, 937 North Harbor Drive, San Diego, CA 92132-0058, 999 555-0002, permission to contact.

ADMINISTRATION FOR THE NAVAL AIR STATION: Chief advisor to the Commanding Officer and Executive Officer and clearinghouse for virtually all administrative problems; personnel, budget, training, awards, travel, manpower needs, telecommunications, security, incoming and outgoing correspondence. Directly supervise sixteen, 16, military and civilian employees, including a supervisor in support of an organization consisting of 1,300 employees.

SUPPORT SERVICES: Direct the administration and management of comprehensive support services including visual information, Naval messages, records, directives, forms and reports, mail operations, building management, graphics, command history, command mission and functions statements, military manning, printing and distribution, classified information, personnel security and military personnel programs.

PROGRAM OPERATIONS OVERSIGHT: Review, analyze, and audit performance of administrative programs to ensure compliance with higher echelon policies and regulations. Evaluate findings and recommendations; develop plans of action and milestones to incorporate needed improvements to correct deficiencies. Direct the overall coordination of command-wide programs including efficiency reviews, awards, dignitary visits, change of command, and command inspections. Casualty Assistance Calls Officer, CACO, Program Manager, as Commander, Navy Region Southwest Sub-Area coordinator for a four county area.

BUDGET FORMULATION AND EXECUTION: Justify and monitor the administrative support services budget. Develop short-range financial requirements in support of the annual Operations and Maintenance Budget in excess of $390,000. Project long-range financial requirements in support of the Program Objectives Memorandum, POM, and Five-Year Defense Plan, FYDP.

INTERNAL SECURITY: Command Security Manager for the Command's Information and Personnel Security Program directing subordinate level Command Deputy Security Managers; classified information and material control, personnel security, security education, emergency plans, security violations and compromises, classification management, security review of information proposed for public release, security records and foreign travel. Assist with the Command's Communication Security Material Control System.

OFFICIAL MAIL CENTER: Provide U. S. accountable mail, guard-mail distribution and collection services for the station and tenant activities. Coordinate operations with the U. S. Postal Service and provide postal directory service for military personnel attached to, or based at, the Station. Monitor the annual postal budget of $155,000.

EMPLOYEE TRAINING: Arrange and schedule required training. Project needs based on hiring, promotion, and other technology and position changes impacting employees' responsibilities. Balance needs consistent with allocated budget to assure fair and equitable distribution of training opportunities to eligible population, and to maximize human resource advantage and effectiveness in accomplishing the mission by targeting training funds according to demonstrated needs and program priorities.

TRAVEL MANAGEMENT: Plan and execute the Command's military and civilian temporary duty travel program to include Command's master temporary duty travel budget formulation, in excess of $260,000; reports, records, preparing and liquidating travel orders, travel arrangements and Government Travel Card Program.

MANPOWER MANAGEMENT: Coordinate the Command's military manpower management system. Assure FYDP data accurately reflects budgeted end-strength, billet requirements and authorizations and accuracy of the Command's Enlisted Distribution and Verification Report and Officer Distribution Control Report.

PERSONNEL, HUMAN RESOURCES: Provide leadership and integration of the Command's diverse military personnel programs including leave, awards, officer requirements, advancement, humanitarian separation, performance evaluations, commissioning, entitlements, educational programs, transfer programs and personnel assignments.

How to Write Your Descriptions

Now that you have an outline of your current or most significant work experience, you have to write about your job responsibilities. You have choices about how you are going to fill in your outline. You can just keep writing a first draft, or you can start choosing sentences and language from your last application form. Here are some directions to help you write your descriptions:

1. **Start writing.** You can simply write about what you do in each of your functional areas. You don't have to make it sound great right now. Just get it on paper. This is a first draft. That's one of the tricks of writing anything — just write! It's easier to rewrite and edit what you have already written. So if you can write about what you do as a contract administrator or manager, simply write it.

   A Visual Information Specialist who also does purchasing was writing his resume. I asked him what kind of job he was seeking now and he said, "Purchasing Agent." I asked him what he had written about his responsibilities in purchasing. He said, "Purchase office supplies and equipment for the office." I told him to write about who his customers were and how much his spending authority was; how he researches products and vendors; and the kind of contracts he wrote. Then I said, why don't you just write down what you do when you purchase something. He said okay. When he rewrote it, his writing showed he was doing exactly the Printing Agent duties!

2. **Think logically and write it all.** Write about what you do undereach skill area thoroughly. You can edit later.

   If you are an e-mail manager, remember all of the elements of your work. Remember that in fact, you installed a new e-mail system for 300 people. You set up the strategy and process for implementing the new software and consulted with users on saving files. You established a one-hour training program for all new users. As a result, e-mail utilization under the new system is more efficient than the previous program. If you don't write it down, your skills bucket won't include these skills.

3. **Refer to your existing resume,** application forms, the SF-171, 612, merit promotion forms, position descriptions, and classification standards to see the language and descriptions. You may find accomplishments and good statements that are usable in the new resume. Read the underlined text in this

paragraph. This is an accomplishment that needs to be expanded. Establishing a new CIO office is a major achievement.

Director of the NETPDTC Customer Service Center, Great Lakes, and Assistant Chief of Staff for MIS for the NTC Commander. Direct computer support and service to the NAVEDTRACOM activities at the NTC complex. Manage requirements definition and coordinate and resolve mission oriented system problems with CDA as well as network and operations support for access to WWW, email, STASS, STASS-RTM and NITRAS. Served on the CNET Strategic workshop, which resulted in a recommendation of the establishment of the CNET Chief Information Officer –CIO- office. Design strategic plans, configuration management, systems integration and server management for over 50 network and corporate database servers, inventory management, ADP security, and ADP acquisition and procurement. Direct supervision of 12 civil servants and Task Manager for 40+ contractors.

4. **Borrow from vacancy announcements and other sources.** Find vacancy announcements that are written well and borrow keywords and phrases from the duties and responsibilities section for your resume. You can find excellent language and descriptions from the vacancy announcements. I was looking for some good language for an Education Specialist and found this vacancy announcement for a Distance Learning Program Manager on the Navy Northeast Web site (www.donhr.navy.mil). This is an outstanding vacancy announcement written in "real words." I've underlined the excellent terminology that could be used in an education specialist, training specialist, or education-related professional's resume.

This position is located in the College of Continuing Education (CCE), Naval War College, Newport, RI. CCE is organized to develop and deliver quality graduate-level, joint professional military educational programs through a variety of delivery methodologies and in a number of geographical locations. The incumbent is responsible for executing the establishment of all approved off-site seminar locations, ensuring the maintenance of the facilities at each remote nonresident seminar site. Periodically visits various nonresident sites, to conduct inventories, establish new programs and/or to troubleshoot/correct logistical problems at existing sites. Serves as CCE's public affairs spokesperson and key marketer to promote CCE's educational opportunities. Manages and facilitates faculty recruitment for both full time and adjunct faculty. Ensures preparation of all advertisements and appropriate documentation. Serves as <u>Contracting Officers Representative</u> to develop <u>Statements of Work, negotiate</u> and coordinate all aspects of each adjunct faculty contract including <u>contract modifications.</u> Prepares and delivers <u>computer generated graphics briefs to depict analysis results.</u> Manages the assignments of all students to seminars and/or correspondence course cohort groups. Coordinates the use of the <u>Video-teleconferencing technology to support lectures, class sessions, and faculty meetings.</u>

5. **Now start writing.** You've done your outline. You're trying to think logically. You have your previous applications nearby. You've looked up vacancy announcements. You've looked at other resume work experience sections. No more excuses.

* Write a brief description of each function. It's okay to make it long and detailed to start, you can always edit and rewrite the text.

* Combine any headings or functions that are repetitive.

* Write 3 to 7 paragraphs or functions for your most important job description

* Previous positions should not be as extensive; one to three paragraphs, plus relevant accomplishments is the maximum length required.

* Use available written materials to fill in your outline. Position descriptions if they are fairly current, past employment forms, resumes, and vacancy announcement text that you have researched.

The next section, "What have you accomplished lately?" will encourage you to remember your accomplishments, in addition to your duties and responsibilities. So keep your accomplishments in the back of your mind as you fill in the outline of your work experience.

One More Example for Extra Inspiration

Here is the current work experience write-up of a Computer Specialist. He has followed the outline format with nouns at the beginning of each paragraph to improve readability. You will see that he is using ALL CAPS and reasonable length paragraphs to make his resume readable. Since you cannot use bold, italics, underlining, or other formatting features in the electronic resume, you can use caps and white space (returns) to improve the look of the resume. This is an easy-to-read and impressive resume, don't you think?

Experience

October 1995 to Present; 40 hours per week; COMPUTER SPECIALIST, GS-0334-13; $49,780 per year; Defense Information Systems Agency, DCTF Slidell; 1010 Gause Boulevard, Slidell, LA 70458; Mr. Jeff Gibbs, (444) 444-4444, may contact.

LIFE CYCLE MANAGER (LCM) of computer systems, business and strategic planning, business and disaster recovery planning, and management of computer centers operations, administration, budget, acquisition and human resources. Developed procedures and plans for opening and operating DISA's Continuity of Operations and Test Facility in Slidell, LA. Team Leader guiding employee transition from large mainframe environments to customer-oriented client/server workstation environment. Project Manager: developed, maintained, and monitored integrated reporting systems for project management and effective evaluation of program operations and milestones.

ACTING HEAD OF THE TEST DIVISION in 1995: Led successful creation of Continuity of Operations capability for the 16 Defense MegaCenters (DMCs). Built prototype site for the Global Combat Support Systems and their integration with the Defense Information Infrastructure Common Operating Environment (DII COE) as supervisor and mentor for seven computer specialists. Assisted commanders with facility, personnel, and operations development. Recovery Consultant: analyzed recovery processes for customers in a fee-for-service environment.

In August 1996, became FIRST DCTF SLIDELL LIAISON REPRESENTATIVE to DISA Headquarters in Washington, DC. Coordinated and integrated management and technical aspects of the DCTF data processing and test mission with administrative matters including standards management, acquisition and configuration management, ADP security, budget, and risk management. Represented DCTF Slidell at all levels within DISA Headquarters. Led team for distributing DISA's COE to customers worldwide. Presented briefings to DISA Director on issues affecting mission and success of Slidell facility. Consulted with private sector contractors in developing information system technology for the government. Completed agency's initial Information Systems Security Certification and procedures to increase information assurance.

Promoted to TEAM LEADER for Strategic Planning & Web Support while continuing role as Lead Command Duty Officer. Supervised team developing Agency Strategic Plan, Disaster Recovery Plan, Facilities Five-Year Plan and other security system designs. Coordinated effort to develop performance measures that cut across organizational boundaries.

MEMBER, CONFIGURATION CONTROL BOARD to ensure proper configuration management. Due to medical emergency, fulfilled duties for the Division Head of the Management Support Division (GM-14) Jun to Oct 98.

PRINCIPAL AUTHOR of comprehensive Organizational Assessment (OA), under auspices of National Performance Review, for the DISA IG. Headed the effort to gather documentation and analysis, process flows, and standard operating procedures. Coordinated publication of a comprehensive report. DCTF Slidell received a good rating from the DISA IG. Received substantial Award and recognition for managing the OA process. Consultant to other Agencies in OA development as a result of outstanding research, publication and organizational system.

Section Review

Writing your work experience description is the most difficult part of the resume. Allow two to four hours to write about your current work experience. Allow additional time to write your other job descriptions. Refer to existing applications and resumes to get content and ideas for writing your resume. Research good language and key words from vacancy announcements that can enhance your resume. Write about what you really do.

D. WHAT HAVE YOU ACCOMPLISHED LATELY?

*Your accomplishments will make your resume
stand apart from your competition*

Have you ever said to yourself, "That was an accomplishment!" If so, you finished something. You achieved a goal, solved a problem, or started something new and saw it through. An accomplishment is the fulfillment of action — getting it done. Anything you do and finish successfully is an accomplishment.

Hiring managers want to know what you've accomplished. Every employee has certain job responsibilities that are expected, but certain accomplishments are not in your position description. Now that you have created an outline of your job responsibilities and filled in the outline, add a few accomplishments to make sure your resume stands out from your competition. You can blend your achievements with your outline or highlight your accomplishments after the general description.

People have a difficult time recognizing, remembering, and writing about their accomplishments. A contract specialist remembered that she negotiated a very challenging contract that involved attorneys for both sides and a difficult sole-source contractor. In spite of the complexity of the contract, she negotiated a win-win contract for both government and the vendors worth $35 million. This is an accomplishment!

Step 4. Add your accomplishments

WORK EXPERIENCE

ACCOMPLISHMENTS: Computerized administrative functions of the office. Acquired hardware and software to create paperless processes over a four-year period. Scanned hard copy files into electronic databases and managed information through a local area network, LAN, system. Resulting increased efficiencies and streamlining enabled us to eliminate three positions, accomplished through normal attrition. Restructured staff functions and responsibilities to reflect new work processes.

Built NT system, resulting in a paperless operation. Print weekly planning bulletin sent electronically, avoiding the expense of printing and time spent sorting and delivering mail.

Teamwork: Fostered cooperative efforts and team approach to analyzing operations and developing options for improvement. Worked with the supervisor from each section, challenged them to look at better ways to plan and deliver services. All recommendations were adopted. Experienced no problems implementing changes due to commitment and buy-in from team members participating in the decision making process.

The Results of Projects Are Accomplishments

Are you a member of a team? Does your team have a project? When you finish this project, it is an accomplishment. Writing about the project's challenge and results will impress the hiring manager and make you stand out! Even if in the planning stages or the project is ongoing, there are milestones of achievement during the life of a project. For instance, achieving funding, approval for the project, maintaining a schedule, and gaining cooperation from team members and customers are all noteworthy milestones and accomplishments in themselves.

Here are some of the elements of a good project list:

* Your role or title

* The name of the project

* The budget

* A description or challenge of the project

* Your actions

* RESULTS

* Awards, recognition, or quotation from a letter saying "thanks."

Info Challenge: The obstacles and challenges of a project? What did you overcome to complete your project.

Results: What happened? Did you save money and time? Are processes now more efficient?

Challenge and Results Examples

The following are some examples that include the challenge and the results, which will keep the hiring manager's interest to the point that you could get hired. You can read more accomplishments in the samples on the CD-ROM with this book. By the way, the acronyms are acceptable here since they were spelled out in the resume — which you'll see on the CD-ROM.

Senior Scientist

Developed a "METOC Support CONOPS for JSIMS," incorporating the Navy's METOC concept of operations. Organized and supervised the planning and execution of two data collection M&S requirements surveys that were conducted in parallel for the military and Joint services. One survey task identified and defined the requirements for atmospheric and near-space data for 75 models and simulations. The other survey task documented existing environmental database capabilities available from 25 Federal Government sources. Our team managed the technical and fiscal activities of four man-years associated with these tasks.

Program Manager/Information Technology Project

Designed a complex, automated, Web telephone system – Info-Works for the Chief of Naval Education and Training (CNET)'s five major training programs. This first-of-a-kind telephone system is accessed by thousands of military personnel seeking training and certification status and programs. Designed the survey to determine what training information is required by users. Researched vendors, analyzed costs, and made a vendor selection (AT&T). Designed the logic flowcharts, options and information to be gathered in the system in cooperation with the AT&T programmer. Wrote multiple scripts and decision trees. Successfully got the program up and running within an established deadline of six months. Wrote a turnover package, including documentation, scripts and materials for the customers.

RESULTS: This system replaced hundreds of daily telephone calls that required human intervention to access a database in order to retrieve information for the callers. Thousands of students/instructors have accessed their information in order to review the status of their application/selection and training status since the inception of the program two years ago. Implementation was September 1997.

Computer Specialist

Designed the master plan for fiber optics for the Marine Base at Albany, GA. Analyzed buildings and facilities for the construction of the overall network architecture so that new technologies could be installed and monitored. Systems to be monitored included: fire protection, security, intrusion detection systems, and audio systems for conferences. The Master Plan was successfully completed and I wrote and gave a briefing before senior Marine Corps officials and Congress. Results: a $5 million budget is planned for the installation of a fiber optics network at the Albany Marine Corps Base.

Librarian

Project Manager, Library Barcoding Project. Supervised the bar-coding of more than 30,000 titles. Planned methods to achieve full automation of the Marine Corps Logistics Base Library. Operated the latest computer-based technology to accomplish this challenging assignment, which will bring the Base Library up-to-date with other public libraries and allow for "virtual" sharing of catalogue information with other libraries off Base. The project is currently at 90% completion. The results will be accessible to the library database via computer, base-wide.

Financial Analyst

Facilitator of the Integrated Product Team (IPT) with 19 members and principal systems analysts for the Base's 1999 Financial Certification. Analyzed the financial situation and discovered deficiencies and bottlenecks. Recognized that critical problems originally occurred when information was transferred from stock control to the new financial system. Items were coded into incorrect accounts. Cooperated with DFAS and Marine Corps Headquarters to target action items and create a milestone chart for a one-year study and improvements. Through the work of the IPT, we successfully achieved the first certification in five years for the base.

Secretary (Office Automation)

Project Leader and sole processor for the redesign, creation and conversion of 39 editorial assistance and subject matter expert templates from Word Perfect 5.1 (DOS) to Word 97. Analyzed WP formatting codes; restructured codes; redesigned, reproduced and improved templates. Trained the professional staff in the use of the new templates. Wrote user-friendly training materials to support new templates. Completed the project in 200 hours to the satisfaction of more than 20 professional program managers and instructors. Received an On-the-Spot award for outstanding performance for completing the project on time and with better design features than previous templates. The citation accompanying the award stated: "Leann was amazing in her ability to convert difficult WP templates into user-friendly and graphically-pleasant templates for staff use."

Course Correspondence Clerk

Developed and wrote the standing operating procedures (SOP) for remote ordering of training courses for sea cadets. Wrote a new set of standards and improved regulations on timelines for ordering courses. Created a new system of ordering correspondence courses. Through the procedure I developed, we drastically reduced the problems with losing training course orders. Served as the sole contact for ordering, with improved control. As a result of the new ordering system, we are now able to review past orders and eliminate duplicate orders. I also established training methods for using the ordering system. Estimated savings per year have been approximately $500,000 for worldwide orders of course materials.

Voucher Examiner

Redesigned the military tuition assistance process program accessed by more than 40,000 military members. The objective of the redesign effort was to streamline procedures for more efficiency, while being able to improve tracking and funds control. During my tenure in this position, the entire computer system for education and training has changed. Over a ten-year period, the system has transitioned from a centralized to a decentralized system, with more autonomy given to local training offices. I have provided technical assistance, troubleshooting, and system design consulting throughout these changes.

Credit Card Program Coordinator

Negotiated the terms for converting to the Web-based Citibank credit card system for Base level small purchase transactions. I analyzed the system, consulted with the PAC and cardholders to implement and operate the new system. The challenge in this assignment was to learn the new streamlined system, while training credit card users/holders to effectively use the improved system. The results are: the new system will be fully converted by 2001 and we are projecting a dramatic increase in efficiency, as well as accuracy of accounting for small purchases, significantly less paperwork and better services to customers.

Production Planner

Administrator for the AAV Ram Reliability Services. Plan the availability, maintainability, rebuilt-to-standard maintenance on AAVs for U.S. and foreign military customers. Determine the best way to maintain the equipment for readiness; cooperate with contractors; research and track parts, make decisions concerning defective parts and replacement. Tracked information from engineers and base engineers. Maintain briefing packages, for weekly presentations. Results: Continuously maintain a successful track record of completion of AAV retrofits in 60 days.

Program Analyst - Safety Critical Fast III Representative (FASTENER)

Following a series of national media television programs (e.g. *60 Minutes* and *20/20*) concerning voluminous military parts and perceived defectiveness, I was selected as a member of a special team formed to analyze up to 5,000 different nuts and bolts stored in the Marine Corps parts inventory. Our team performed critical testing and removed weak or damaged fasteners to be utilized with Marine Corps end items. Based on engineering analysis and review of functions, the team determined that only 10 separate varieties of nuts and bolts would do the same job with better results over the long run.

Accounting Specialist

Accountant for a liquidation savings program designed to recover equipment dollars. Produced error reports, located document numbers, notified the administrator and customers to correct pricing errors. By monitoring and follow-up on red-flagged price increases for liquidated products, we were able to recover $60,000 rather than $30,000. Additionally, through our carefully planned approach based on routine follow-up on all price increases originating from other Major Commands, we discovered that certain types of orders needed to be watched very closely for increases in price.

Equipment Specialist

Manage testing equipment for Marine Corps.

As the team leader for the inventory management site, I developed a research program designed to fill large back-orders requesting test equipment. The team developed a comprehensive plan for analyzing existing assets in the equipment warehouse, analyzed quality of test equipment, and developed a detailed repair plan to bring test equipment back up to "A" performance. The primary result of my work was that we were able to fill as many as a third of all back-orders with existing and newly-repaired test equipment, which had previously been stored as unserviceable equipment.

Computer Specialist (Webmaster)

As one of the original team of developers for the Albany Web site, I have managed the growth of the Web site from its 1998 inception to the current size of more than 5,000 pages, contributed by more than 30 Web writers across six agencies, published both for intranet and Internet. The vision and direction of the project has changed from one of information to a strong emphasis on morale building, usability by customers, and overall reliability of the Web site.

Administrative Officer

Computerized administrative functions of the office. Acquired hardware and software to create paperless processes over a four-year period. Scanned hard copy files into electronic databases and managed information through a local area network (LAN) system. Resulting increased efficiencies and streamlining enabled us to eliminate three positions, accomplished through normal attrition. Restructured staff functions and responsibilities to reflect new work processes.

Section Review

Selling yourself with your accomplishments isn't easy, but it's the most important section in your resume. You must try to remember your achievements. If you simply cannot write an accomplishment, or if you haven't been involved in any accomplishments recently, find a new project or challenge in your job so that you can include it in your resume. The sample electronic resumes on the CD-ROM all include accomplishments. Read them and try to think of your accomplishments.

The final section in this chapter, *Putting It All Together,* shows you how to combine your outline, descriptions, and accomplishments into your resume.

 Info
Keep a list of accomplishments for your resume. Give a copy of your list to your supervisor before your next appraisal.

If you haven't accomplished anything particular for the last couple of years, you REALLY need to write your resume so that you can find a new job!

E. WHAT HAPPENED TO YOUR KSAS?

With the electronic resume application system, you must include your knowledge, skills, and abilities in your work experience descriptions.

The new "resume + data sheet only" announcements and application processes no longer require that you write separate KSAs. But the hiring managers still want to know what knowledge, skills, and abilities you have that will show your skill level and ability to perform a job.

Vacancy announcements are all different when it comes to describing the knowledge, skills, and abilities needed for each job.

When the announcement requests a resume only (or resume, plus additional data sheet), the KSAs are to be described within the text of your work experience.

Example 1 — U.S. Navy Vacancy Announcement

This is a SW Navy vacancy announcement that lists the knowledge, skills, and abilities desired for this job. The instructions for applying for the job tell the applicant to submit only the resume and additional data sheet. In this case, you would cover the KSA information in the text of your work experience. The knowledge, skills, and abilities are written in three areas of the announcement:

1. Duties

2. Qualifications

3. Knowledge, skills, and abilities

Look for the KSAs so that you are sure to cover them in the resume.

Visual Information Specialist — SW Navy Announcement

Duties:

This series includes positions that supervise or perform work involved in communicating information through visual means. Work in this series includes the design and display of such visual materials as photographs, illustrations, diagrams, graphs, objects, models, slides, and charts used in books, magazines, pamphlets, exhibits, live or video recorded speeches or lectures, and other means of communicating. The work requires knowledge of and ability to apply the principles of visual design; knowledge of the technical characteristics associated with various methods of visual display; and the ability to present subject matter information in a visual form that will convey the intended message to, or have the desired effect on, the intended audience.

Qualifications:

ADDITIONAL REQUIREMENTS: Education: Undergraduate and Graduate Education: Major study - commercial art, fine arts, or art history, industrial design, architecture, drafting, interior design, photography, visual communication or other fields related to the position. Some positions may require subject-matter knowledge of medicine, science, or technical equipment.

KSAs:

<u>Knowledge of and ability</u> to apply the principles of visual design. Knowledge of the technical characteristics associated with the various methods of visual display. Ability to present subject matter information in a visual form that will convey the intended message to, or have the desired effect on, the intended audience.

How to apply:

You may submit your resume and your responses to the questions on the Additional Data Sheet by e-mail (preferred) or by U.S. mail. By e-mail: E-mail your resume in the body of your message. Do not send as an attachment. Submit to wantajob@sw.hroc.navy.mil. By U.S. mail: HRSC-SW, Attn: Code 53, 525 B Street, Suite 600, San Diego, CA 92101-4418. If submitting your resume by e-mail, do not send anything other than your resume and your responses to the Additional Data Sheet questions.

Example 2 — U.S. Army Vacancy Announcement

This is an Army resume inventory-building announcement that is very short and general. The Specialized Experience paragraph tells you that the KSAs are typical for this position. The Army has a PD Library on the Web site, so the PD information for this position is listed here as well. The knowledge, skills, and abilities are available in the PD. Another way to find the KSAs for Personnel Specialist is to look for other vacancy announcements in this series that still list KSAs. You would apply for this position with a resume and supplemental sheet only.

Personnel Specialist — U.S. Army

Duties: Personnel Management Specialist (Generalist), GS-0201: Advises on, supervises, performs or provides staff leadership and technical guidance for work in any two civilian personnel functions, i.e. Position Classification, Employee Development, Staffing Assistance and Recruitment, and Management Employee Relations.

Specialized Experience: Experience that equipped the applicant with the particular knowledge, skills, and abilities (KSAs) to perform successfully the duties of the position, and that is typically in or related to position to be filled.

KSAs: Not applicable - these positions are being filled using RESUMIX procedures. Please visit our home page and read the RESUMIX Job Kit at www.chrma.hqusareur.army.mil

Text from the PD Library at the Army site:

MAJOR DUTIES

Serves as principle assistant to the Director in carrying out a military personnel management program. Advises staff on all technical aspects of the program and researches personnel problems of a more complex nature. A secret clearance is required for this position.

1. Provides technical support to the Director. Advises Commander and subordinate Commanders in all technical aspects of the military personnel function. Applies an intimate knowledge of the basic concepts and theories of personnel management in addressing all actions directed to the Military Personnel Division. Evaluates the military personnel programs from a technical status, deficiencies, and makes recommendations on same. 50%

2. Provides technical guidance and control over the four major areas of the Military Personnel program. 15%

a. Records: Audits official military personnel files (officer and enlisted) Ensures that correct procedures have applied and that files are complete. Insures that discrepancies are corrected. 10%

b. Management: Reviews all reassignments for proper documentation and correct substantive processing (e.g., sponsorship arranged, qualification, MOS, rank, time in service remaining, reenlistment requirements, etc.). 15%

c. Actions: Ensures all personnel actions (e.g., compassionate reassignment, tour extensions, suspension of favorable action, etc.) are accomplished correctly and in a timely manner. 10%

Example 3 — Navy SE Vacancy Announcement

This SE Navy announcement is still requesting KSAs to be written on separate pages. You can use your electronic resume plus the KSAs to apply for this job. If you have your resume in a database already, you could self-nominate by email and send the KSAs in the text box of the email. Soon, these types of announcements will be eliminated so that the KSAs will be blended into the resume text. For this particular announcement, keeping the KSAs separate would be wise. You could call and ask the SE center if the KSAs can be blended into the resume, but you might have difficulty getting somebody on the phone. You could write and ask. It's possible that if you did a good job, they could be combined with the resume. That is the style of the future.

Info Blend your statements regarding your knowledge, skills, and abilities for each of your career areas into your resume.

Management Assistant (OA), GS-334-9

Knowledge, Skills, and Abilities:

Applicants meeting basic eligibility requirements will be rated and ranked on the knowledge, skills, and abilities (KSAs) and other characteristics required to perform the duties of the position. The KSAs are listed below. Include in the write-ups such things as experience in and out of Federal Service that gave you the specific knowledge, skill, or ability; objectives of your work and evidence of your success (such as accomplishments, awards received, etc.) 1. Knowledge of military personnel policies, precedents, regulations and procedures. 2. Knowledge of personal computers and software such as word processors, graphics, spreadsheets, database management systems, etc. 3. Ability to prepare and/or edit written correspondence, ensuring proper use of English grammar, spelling and punctuation. 4. Ability to review and maintain records.

Evaluation Method:

Candidates should submit a narrative statement on a separate page(s) with specific responses to the knowledge, skills, and abilities (KSAs) in this announcement. Failure to submit your narrative response to the KSAs for this job may affect your eligibility and/or rating negatively for this position.

How Do You Include the KSAs in the Text of Your Work Experience?

By writing a good description of your work. By following the instructions for resume writing in the *Hats, Nouns, and Skills* section of this chapter. By creating an outline of your experience (and skills), you are going to cover your knowledge, skills, and abilities. You do have to think about the KSAs for the jobs, however. The following work experience section covers the KSAs for this job.

Example 4 — Resume Excerpt: Realty Specialist, GS-1170-7

This resume excerpt is from Ron's Realty Specialist resume. Compare the resume experience write-up to the PD description from the Army PD library. You will see the knowledge, skills, and abilities written in the PD. They are clearly covered in the experience section of the resume.

December 1998 to Present. 40 hours per week, REALTY SPECIALIST (GS-1170-07-01). US Army Corps of Engineers, 1325 J Street, Sacramento, CA 95814, Dan Kelly, Supervisor (916) 557-7115. Analyze and gather preliminary real estate data from multiple sources, including: installation commanders, real estate brokers, Board of Realtors, Assessors Office, MLS services. Conduct studies on the impact of military installation closures/realignments (BRAC) on the local real estate markets.

Negotiate and administer lease agreements between other government agencies and DoD for the transfer of real property. Perform on-site property inspections on the conditions of single-family residences and commercial leased properties prior to government acquisition/leasing; identifying areas of concern prior to government action.

Prepare written replies to Homeowners Assistance Program applicants who appeal their denial of benefits, simplifying the legal terms and giving the applicants a clearer understanding and description for their denial. Demonstrate knowledge of Public Law 91-646. Compose Rights of Entry and determine real property ownership through investigation of Assessor's records and tax rolls to notify land owners of pending government action (i.e. ordnance removal, etc.). Develop and maintain complex spreadsheets for financial, workload trends and tracking in Excel, Quattro Pro, and Lotus.

Realty Specialist, Position Description from the Army PD Library

1. Acquisition Actions. (75%)

Negotiates with owners and their representatives to obtain interests in real estate. Takes necessary actions to complete the acquisition or the required real estate interest, including ensuring that needed support documents, instruments, agreements, maps, appraisals, title policies, and closing services are available and present as required. Explains to owners and their representatives how values are determined. Analyzes title reports to determine what steps are needed to be taken to meet DA and Department of Justice requirements for titles.

2. Correspondence. (25%)

Prepares all correspondence required in the acquisition process, including leases, offers, deeds, rights of entries, affidavits, subordinations, etc. Applies knowledge of Public Law 91-646 and amendments to ensure acquisition is conducted properly and that owners are given proper information regarding their relocation benefits.

FACTOR 1, KNOWLEDGE REQUIRED BY THE POSITION

- Knowledge of the COE's acquisition policies and regulation requirements.

- Ability to review documents provided by others to ensure CoE and Federal Relocation Services policies and procedures are met.

- Knowledge of the mission organization, and work processes of programs throughout the Corps District and the relationship to administrative support activities.

- A thorough knowledge of real estate laws and procedures to read and interpret various maps and surveys.

- Knowledge of Federal laws and regulations as these relate to property acquisition.

- Skill in preparing correspondence and reports.

Research Organizations and Industries for Government or Private Industry

Resume writing for government and, in fact, for private industry requires research and knowledge of the organization's needs. You need to read about the organization and any available material on job requirements. If you wanted a job with Dell Computer, you would go to Dell's Website and read about the company. You would go to their Employment pages and read their recruitment advertisements. You would also investigate the knowledge, skills, and abilities required for the job. You would also look at the particular language they use when they write about their jobs. If you really wanted to work for Dell, you would include some of their words in your work experience descriptions. After all, you want to look like you belong there.

Using industry language and covering the desired qualifications of the hiring organization is not a new concept with the "resume only" application process. Savvy job applicants have been researching organizations, industry language, and philosophy for years. It just seems more important now that the agencies are using artificial intelligence to analyze your resume for your knowledge, skills, abilities, and qualifications. The human personnel specialist is not going to analyze, assume, or guess that you have certain skills and are qualified when you said one thing that implies another. Nowadays, if your resume doesn't spell out the specific knowledge, skills, abilities, and industry language, the computer is not going to find you. It's a much more cut-and-dried approach. The right words have to be in the resume. You have to do some research to find the words, and the Internet is easy to use for this purpose.

Example 5 — Case Study from Private Industry: Corporate Trainer

Deborah is seeking a career change into corporate training. She is currently a teacher and case manager for emotionally disturbed high school students. Deborah researched the industry language (keywords), knowledge, skills, and abilities for a Corporate Trainer. She rewrote her resume with the language of the industry. Let's follow the steps she took to accomplish this.

Step 1: Deborah drafted her resume as she normally would as a teacher.

WORK EXPERIENCE DRAFT (partial):

Teacher, trainer, Baltimore County Public Schools, 1982 to present

Plan for students and instructional assistants. Maintain ongoing student data and relate data to team members. Develop and create lesson plans for students. Maintain student records. Manage, train, and maintain staff development. Assess and measure student growth and progress. Organize student records.

Maryland State Teacher's Association, 1998 to 1999

Trainer – Facilitator - Women's Leadership Training

Step 2: Deborah began searching the Internet for corporate trainer keywords.

Deborah went to the Internet to find companies that were in her geographic region where they hire corporate trainers. She needed to know how to write about training, instead of teaching in a public school system. She found three companies easily and printed out their recruitment advertisements. Two are listed here.

1. **Lucent.com — Global Learning Solutions**. Corporate mission: Global Learning Solutions is moving into e-learning solutions that would allow us to train more associates and customers faster while holding down expenses.

   Recruitment ad: Instructional Systems Designer. Qualified candidates must have the ability to prepare training materials, job aid plans, practical exercises, performance evaluation criteria, and work directly with clients. Seeking 2 years of stand-up training experience.

2. **Marriott Corporation.** IR Trainer Recruitment ad: Develop skills to provide training to business clients. Coordinate training programs. Identify potential solutions to business training problems. Become familiar with customer priorities, critical systems and key contacts. Identify potential solutions to busi ness training problems.

Step 3: Deborah rewrote her resume using the language from the recruitment ads and corporate descriptions. Deborah's entire resume is located on the CD-ROM in the Private Industry Resume Section.

The new resume includes the desired KSAs plus the industry language. The resume emphasizes communications skills, curriculum development, instructional design, problem solving, customer relations and consulting with customers. She realizes she does that as a teacher and as a volunteer trainer for her teacher's union.

The "Expertise" section is a summary of skills that can be written in a summary paragraph (called "Other Information" for the Navy Resume Builder).

EXPERTISE

* Professional Training Topics: Educational, including Computer Skills, Teamwork, Decision-Making, Accepting Change, Organizational Development, and Problem solving.

* Curriculum designs consider business processes, critical systems, organizational objectives, skills, and competency levels.

* Materials development: Presentation materials, instructional support materials, exercises, agenda, course descriptions, marketing, and promotional materials.

* Technical writing, editing, and materials production.

* Consult and recommend training solutions to achieve organizational change and corporate/educational goals.

* Strategic planning and communications to achieve training, customer and student learning goals within established schedules and deadlines.

* Adaptable and flexible in stand-up teaching environment involving unique teaching situations, travel, and unknown variables.

PROFESSIONAL TEACHING EXPERIENCE

Teacher, Western School of Technology   1999 to present

Teacher, Woodmoore Elementary Schools   1993 to 1999

Develop and implement curriculum; assess performance and learning levels; and create tools for teaching. Utilize writing, editing, communications, listening, and problem-solving skills. Curriculum includes basic Internet, Windows, and Microsoft software product curriculum. Professional team member working to achieve instructional goals for special needs students. Demonstrate interpersonal skills and creativity to develop curriculum and methods of teaching to meet unique learning processes for students.

Computers: In-depth knowledge of Office 97; learn new applications quickly; Print Shop Deluxe 6.0 for producing worksheets and print instruction materials.

Section Review

Don't forget your KSAs completely just because the application requirements have changed. For the new "resume only" announcements, cover your KSAs in your work experience section.

The knowledge, skills, and abilities that demonstrate your ability to perform a certain job should still be considered and covered in your resume. They will never disappear for human resources and hiring managers who are always looking for your KSAs. It's their second nature to look for your KSAs. For many years KSAs got a bad name because of the huge amount of effort that went into writing one page of copy for each KSA required. That was laborious and unnecessary. If you simply remember your KSAs for your various career interests and integrate them into your resume, you will be successful with the database searches, as well as the impression you make on the hiring manager.

The final section in this chapter is entitled *Putting It All Together* and gives you an outline for writing your Work Experience write-ups. We'll discuss how to include your duties, responsibilities, accomplishments, and KSAs in a couple of succinct paragraphs.

F. PUTTING IT ALL TOGETHER

Until all of the Work Experience resume sections are compiled together and edited, you cannot begin marketing yourself to your next career — or apply for a new job.

CD-ROM Electronic Resume Samples

In order to stay focused and put your resume together, you should see what a good electronic resume looks like. This would be a good time to go to the CD-ROM to review the sample electronic resumes. The 18 sample electronic resumes on the CD-ROM demonstrate my instructions from various chapters in the book.

Skills Extraction and Your Skills Bucket — The Resumix samples include keywords and skills for the job series. We cannot guarantee these resumes contain all of the perfect keywords, but we did our research.

One Resume Fits All — The samples are written for multiple job series and interests. We have researched keywords for multiple series.

Hats, Nouns, and Skills — The work experience descriptions are written in small paragraphs with each paragraph focusing on a particular functional skill area. Look for the words in ALL CAPS.

Filling in Your Outline — The description of duties has been written based on position descriptions, language found in vacancy announcements, and new content written to describe the jobs.

What Have You Accomplished Lately? — The resume accomplishments are included clearly after the description of job duties. Want to stand out? Include accomplishments.

What Happened to Your KSAs? — The knowledge, skills, and abilities are included in the descriptions of their jobs.

Plain Language Resumes — The samples, written in the active voice with limited use of the personal pronoun *I*, are succinct, sentences are varied in length, and verbs are consistent. The style of writing is concise, yet informative and interesting.

Dos and Don'ts — The samples follow the electronic resume writing standards with the exception of bold type. We have included bold type in our samples to increase your readability. When you copy and paste your text into a resume builder, the boldface type will be eliminated because of the form text limitations.

Real Samples Contributed by Real Civilian Employees

MANAGEMENT ANALYST, GS-343-12

ADMINISTRATIVE OFFICER, GS-341-12

MANAGEMENT/PROGRAM ANALYST, GS-343-12

SENIOR SCIENTIST, GS-XXX-14

SHORE SITE INSTALLATION MANAGER/EQUIPMENT SPECIALIST, GS-1670-12

INSTRUCTIONAL SYSTEM SPECIALIST, GS-1750-12

SYSTEMS ACCOUNTANT, GS-510-12

COMPUTER SPECIALIST, GS-334-13

DIVISION SECRETARY, GS-318-4

LOCKSMITH, ELECTRONICS, WG

WRITER/EDITOR, GS-1082

ELECTRICAL ENGINEER, GS-850-11

REALTY SPECIALIST, GS-1170-7

EDUCATION SERVICES GUIDANCE COUNSELOR, GS-1740-9

SUPERVISORY CONTRACT SPECIALIST, GS-1102-14

LOGISTICS SPECIALIST, GS-034-5

INVENTORY MANAGEMENT SPECIALIST, GS-2010-7

SECRETARY, GS-318-5

Chapter 10

The Resume Builder and Other Information

Use a Resume Builder to submit your resume to the agency databases. Copy and paste your resume into the Resume Builders from your word-processed file.

What is a Resume Builder?

A Resume Builder is a form that you fill out in order to submit your resume to a human resources office. There are many Resume Builders. There are different Builders for Army, Navy, Air Force, and all of the employers in private industry. Every organization has its own Builder. That's why you need to write your resume in a word processing program and be ready to copy and paste the resume into each of the Builders.

The Resume Builder is not the resume database. The Builder is the method of submitting the resume into the database. If you ever find that you cannot access your resume because a Builder is down, this does not mean your resume has been erased from a database, it simply means that the Builder is down. Return at a later time and retrieve and edit your resume.

Resume Builder Samples

Most of the Resume Builders are similar. This chapter includes abstracts of the Navy Resume Builder so that you can visualize the fields and read the instructions that are written within the Resume Builder. These sections are fairly self-explanatory. You can see many examples of content for these sections in the 18 sample Resumix resumes on the CD-ROM. You can find directions to help you locate the various Resume Builders in Chapter 3, "Job Kits Made Easier."

How to Use the Resume Builder and Self-Nominate

Write your resume in your favorite word processing software. Then copy and paste the text into the major fields. You should proofread and use the spellchecker before copying and pasting the text because Resume Builder does not include a spellchecker. Most of the Builders have "required fields" that have to be filled in before you san SAVE your work. After you fill out the required fields (usually personnel-related questions and important personal information, such as name, address, e-mail), you can save the form, and return at a later time to complete the Builder. After you are finished, be sure to hit SUBMIT so that you actually apply for a job, if that is your wish.

Sometimes people simply fill out the Resume Builder before they actually find a job for which they are interested. That way the resume is in the database before the announcement is posted. After you find an announcement, you simply self-nominate for that job by e-mail or a special self-nominate button. The Air Force has an excellent self-nomination form; the Navy is developing a self-nomination link from each announcement; Army uses self-nomination for many announcements. In all of the self-nomination systems, the resume can either be in the database ahead of time, or it can be submitted for a particular position.

Allow enough time in the process. If you are completing a Resume Builder for the first time for a specific announcement and deadline, be sure to leave two or three working days for your copy to reach the human resources office. Do not wait until the last minute, you might lose consideration for the job if the resume isn't actually at the human resource office. Read the directions for how often you need to update your Resume Builder. They are all different.

Why use the Resume Builder instead of submitting your resume by e-mail?

You should submit your resume through the Resume Builder so that you can update your resume. If you take the time to copy and paste your text into the Resume Builders, you will be able to update, change your e-mail addresses, add new projects and additional training classes, and keep your other information relevant and recent.

Be sure to keep your other information relevant. If you completed secretarial training in 1985 and you are now a Program Analyst, GS-12, do not include the secretarial training. If you received an award in high school from 1975, this is probably not relevant (unless it was very distinctive). If you completed welding certification in your first career as a Wage Grade, but now you are a Project Manager, GS-13, the trades certificates will not be as important as your project management training. If you started your career as a Stay-in-School and you're now a GS-9, you could leave the Stay-in-School out of the resume. Keep it relevant to your current situation and goals.

The resume information should also be recent. There is no firm definition of "recent," but the most recent would be within the last five to ten years. If you completed a significant training course in 1985 that has affected your career, you should include that also. Analyze your training and awards list. Focus on the last five to ten years.

Other Information

"Other Information" is all of the other information besides Work Experience. These resume sections include: Personal Information, Education, Training, Awards and Honors, Licenses, Community Service, and interpersonal traits. Listed below is a sample of each section.

I. PERSONAL INFORMATION

Follow the exact format from your Resume Builder. Each of the Job Kits is slightly different. You can use either home or work e-mail. Be sure to type the e-mail address correctly. Use only one e-mail address. If you don't have an e-mail address, leave it blank. They will communicate with you by regular mail. You can update your resume if the e-mail address changes. Type your name in ALL CAPS, as shown in the following example:

ANGELA P. JOHNSON

SSN: 555009876

902 Rocky Road

Denver, CO 88888

Home Phone: (000) 000-0000

Work Phone: (333) 333-3333

E-mail Address: APJohnson@aol.com

II. EDUCATION

Education is very important, as you well know. Many Federal job series require a college degree. Others give you the opportunity to exchange years of specialized experience with a degree. There are usually three to five blocks for different college entries. If you have not finished a degree, just list the number of credit hours completed and the major concentration. List the highest college level first.

College, University or Technical/Vocational School:

City, State, Country (if other than US):

Major:

Year Completed: (Format yyyy)

Type of Degree:

GPA:

Total Credit Hours Earned:

Type:

High School:

City, State, Country:

Year Completed: (Format yyyy)

Diploma or GED equivalent:

Here is an example of a completed education section:

EDUCATION:

MS Business Management, University of Central Texas, Aug 1984

BS Business Administration, University of Central Texas, Aug 1980

AS Fashion Merchandising, Daytona Beach Community College, May 1978

Springfield High School, Springfield, TX, 1975

If you have not finished your degree, write the following information:

University of Maryland Baltimore County, Baltimore, MD, B.S. expected May 2001

Major: Information Technology; 85 credits completed.

III. OTHER WORK-RELATED INFORMATION

If you are a Federal employee who has had extensive training in the past, organize your training list into categories of training. Include the title of your course, classroom hours, and date completed. Include only the most recent courses — those you've completed within the last eight years. If you had important training 10 years ago, include it at your discretion.

Professional Training

List any courses that you have completed and consider relevant to your career goal(s). Please include course name, length, and completion date. You are limited to approximately 1500 characters.

Example: Supervising Civilian Employees, 40 hrs, 1998; Defense Cost and Price Analysis, 80 hrs, 1997.

Here's an example of a completed training section:

TRAINING

FINANCE: Federal Financial Statement & Audit Requirements, OMB and CFO Council Forum, 1998; DFAS Merit Systems Training for Managers, 1998; CFO Financial Statement Reporting, FSAB, 1998; Working Capital Fund, DFAS, 1998; Government Financial Management Instructor Training, 1998

LEADERSHIP: DFAS Staircase Professional Leadership Development Training, 1998; Professional Military Comptrollers Course, 1996

CONTRACTS AND COSTING: Activity Base Costing, 1996; Defense Security Assistance Financial Course, 1995; Financial Managers Staff Officers Course, 1994; US Army Command and General Staff Officer College, 1991; Resource Management Budget, 1992; Federal Appropriations Law, 1992; Management of Defense Contracts, 1990.

COMPUTER APPLICATIONS: Windows (98/NT); Microsoft DOS; MS Word, Excel, PowerPoint, Access, Project.

Licenses and Certifications

This section is very important so be sure to include any license or certification that demonstrates specialized qualifications for your career field.

List current licenses, certificates, and/or contracting warrants. Identify the city and/or state of certification and expiration date, if any. You are limited to approximately 1500 characters.

Example: Certified Public Accountant (CPA), Illinois, 6/95.

If you have Defense Acquisition Workforce Improvement Act (DAWIA) certification, identify the level and position category such as contracting, purchasing, quality assurance, development, or engineering.

Example: DAWIA Level III Certification (Contracting), 8/96.

Here's an example of a completed Licenses and Certificates section:

LICENSES AND CERTIFICATES:

Certified Government Financial Manager, January 1996.

DAWIA, III, Current

Certified Public Accountant

Certified Property Manager

Member, Maryland Court of Appeals, 1995 to present

Licensed Social Worker (LCSW), State of Maryland, 1999

Registered Nurse

Type "C" Driver's License

Secret Clearance, Current

Certified Microsoft Network Engineer, 1999

Hazardous Materials Certificate

Performance Ratings, Awards, Honors, and Recognitions

You will be given points for this category. If you have room to describe why you received a particular award, these statements may add additional skill hits to your resume.

List performance ratings, awards, honors, and recognitions received, including date(s) of receipt. You are limited to approximately 1500 characters.

Example: Outstanding rating 6/99, 6/98; Performance Award 7/99, 8/98; Special Act Award 1/99, 2/98.

Note: Use ENTER for line/paragraph breaks and TAB to proceed to the next block.

Here's an example of a completed Awards and Honors section:

AWARDS AND HONORS:

Sustained Performance/cash awards, 1998, 1997, 1996, 1995, 1994

Outstanding Performance Award, 1995

Secretary of the Army, General Lesley McNair Essay Award and cash award, April 92

Community Service Awards, 1998/1992/1991

Other Information

List any information relevant to your career goal(s). Include publications, language proficiencies, memberships in professional organizations or honor societies, membership in Acquisition Professional Community (ACP), leadership activities, and so forth. You are limited to approximately 1500 characters.

Example: Proficient in Spanish. Typing Speed: 65 wpm. Dictation 80 wpm. Phi Beta Kappa Alumnus. Acquisition Professional Community Member since 1996.

Here are a few examples of information you could include in this section:

* Professional memberships

* Publications

* Presentations

* Courses taught

* Community service and volunteer positions

* Interpersonal skills

* Languages

* Patents

Soft Skills, Interpersonal Skills, Core Competencies, and your "Emotional Intelligence"

Do any of the following characteristics — or "soft skills" — describe you?

a particularly hard worker

flexible

dedicated

able to complete projects on time

handle difficult people easily

negotiate solutions

resolve problems

listen

mentor co-workers

If so, you have skills that may be of interest to a selecting official.

An Excerpt from an Expert

Daniel Goleman writes in *Working with Emotional Intelligence* (Bantam Books, 2000) about What employers want: "A survey of American employers reveals that more than half the people who work for them lack the motivation to keep learning and improving in their job. Four in ten are not able to work cooperatively with fellow employees, and just 19 percent of those applying for entry-level jobs have enough self-discipline in their work habits.

In a national survey of what employers are looking for in entry-level workers, specific technical skills are now less important than the underlying ability to learn on the job. After that, employers listed:

* Listening and oral communication

* Adaptability and creative responses to setbacks and obstacles

* Personal management, confidence, motivation to work toward goals, a sense of wanting to develop one's career and take pride in accomplishments

* Group and interpersonal effectiveness, cooperativeness, and teamwork, skills at negotiating disagreements

* Effectiveness in the organization, wanting to make a contribution, leadership potential

A study of what corporations are seeking in the MBAs they hire yields a similar list. The three most desired capabilities are communications skills, interpersonal skills, and initiative. As Jill Fabule, managing director of admissions and financial aid at the Harvard Business School told me, "empathy, perspective taking, rapport, and cooperation" are among the competencies the school is looking for in those who apply."

Here are a few personal qualities that you may want to list for selecting officials.

Personal Qualities include: flexibility and adaptability, excellent listening capabilities, ability to work hard to complete projects on time, able to handle multiple projects simultaneously, creative in problem-solving.

IV. SUMMARY OF SKILLS

Some Resume Builders have a field where you can summarize your skills. The Summary is an excellent section to add to any resume, including those for private industry. It synopsizes and sells your qualifications and skills to the hiring manager. Here is an example of a Summary of Skills section for an Accountant and Financial Manager. This paragraph is filled with keywords!

SUMMARY OF SKILLS:

Certified Government Financial Manager (CGFM); Systems Accounting; Budget Analysis; Management Analysis; Statistical and analytical processes; Management engineering studies; Organizational reviews; Manpower requirements; Project resource allocations; Workload requirements; IBM compatible computers; Computer based Financial Management software. DOD Secret Security Clearance.

Expert in budget estimates, budget planning, programming, and execution; fund accountability; financial management oversight and reporting. Demonstrated ability in analyzing, evaluating, and implementing DOD Accounting and Financial policies; systems analysis; financial statement preparation and reporting; strategic planning; regulatory compliance; audit reviews and follow-up; internal management control.

Chapter Review

You should have a draft of all of the sections of your resume by now. You have edited and selected relevant and recent training; edited your awards list; written your certifications; and listed your other qualifications, such as community service and interpersonal skills. Congratulations! You are almost finished!

Just two more resume-writing chapters to go before you can copy and paste your resume into the Resume Builders. You can make it!

The next chapter, "Plain Language Resumes," will help you edit your content so that it is written succinctly and in the active voice. The final resume-writing chapter, "Dos and Don'ts for Electronic Resume Writing," will help you format the resume for the Resume Builder, or to submit the resume via e-mail.

Web addresses for the Resume Builders are listed in Chapter 3, "Job Kits Made Easier." The actual job kits with more resume-writing instruction can be found on the CD-ROM of this book.

(i) Info   **Add Your Soft Skills and Emotional Intelligence**

Include your interpersonal traits or "soft skills."
Are you flexible, customer-focused, able to resolve problems?
Do you have initiative and use creativity to meet obstacles?

Part 5

Editing and Formatting Tips

Chapter 11
Plain Language Resumes

Chapter 12
Electronic Resumes Dos and Don'ts

Chapter 11

Plain Language Resumes

How do you look on paper?

It's high time civilians learn to write about their career accomplishments in a concise, clear, and non-bureaucratic writing style. It's past time for civilians to recognize their skills and accomplishments, and even brag a little. A three- to five-page resume does not allow the space to write every little detail of your work. Now you have to select the most important experiences and write the resume in a new writing style — plain language.

 Info A well-written resume will help you get SELECTED for a promotion, increase your salary, and add to your retirement fund. All of the writing and editing effort will pay off!

This chapter might be one of the most important in this book. The ten resume writing principles spelled out in this chapter will result in a well-written, easy-to-read, likable, factual, concise, and marketable resume.

Some federal employees have never written a resume; some have drafted their "best-attempt" resume, but are looking for improvements; others have already written their resumes and want to make sure they have written the best they can. Everyone is at a different point in the process and brings a different writing and editing skill and interest level.

You rely on your resume to make a good first impression on a potential employer — perhaps your only impression. Your resume should certainly say who you are as a professional; but whether you want it to or not, it also says something about you as a person. For example, a long resume may be intended to say that you have accomplished a lot, but it may have the effect of telling the reader that you are long-winded or unfocused. Or, a resume full of lofty language may be intended to say that you are smart, but may reveal to the reader that you are full of hot air. Your hopes of a better job depend on your resume-writing abilities and even your dreams of a happier life. No wonder resumes can seem so hard to write!

But what a difference a good resume makes! Crisp, concise language; strong professional words; clear construction and organization — they all add up to a powerful statement about you.

Civilians haven't given much thought to their resumes in the past because of the SF-171, OF-612, merit promotion forms, and skills codes. Now that it is mandatory to write a good resume, this skill will be critical to your career (unless you are retiring or totally happy in your current job).

Most of us don't give ourselves enough credit in our resumes. Sometimes this is due to misplaced modesty. Sometimes it's because of the "I can't take full credit for that because we do this work as a team" attitude, and that you shouldn't take credit for the team's work. More often, though, it's either a failure to recognize the significance of your performance or an inability to articulate your performance in a way that sounds meaningful.

Consider the following examples.

Example 1:

Responsible for the drafting of important document. Additionally responsible for compiling information and organizing meetings.

Well, that's not enough. It tells us very little. Let's see if we can fix it up some.

Example 2:

Worked with others in the drafting of important documents. Wrote various parts of document and negotiated compromises. Document was later used as starting-point for important experiments in democracy. Worked with senior politicians. Highly positive outcomes resulted.

Better, but are you impressed? Probably not. Try this:

Example 3:

Principal architect of the United States Constitution, the historical blueprint for the first free democracy on earth. Negotiated the liberties of the people with the greatest minds of our time. Built successful coalitions among highly polarized leaders of the future states.

Is that more impressive? All three examples describe the same accomplishment of James Madison, the "Father of the Constitution." Few of us can boast successes on a Madisonian scale; the point is that even his accomplishments sound dull when couched in bureaucratic and stilted phrases.

Fortunately, writing a good resume can be made manageable, simple, and even easy, if you follow a few guidelines. While there's no substitute for experience, even a first-time resume writer can produce a perfectly fine resume. And the more you practice, the better you will become.

To write a good resume, you have to be able to do three things:

* First, you need to be able to write well. Face it: you can't make a good resume out of poor sentences. And you will learn how to write well in these pages. If you work at it, you can do it.

* Second, you need to be able to perceive your abilities and accomplishments clearly and objectively, neither diminished through false modesty nor exaggerated through undue pride.

* Third, you must be able to assemble the well-written and accurate description of your qualifications into a compact, focused package. Chapter 9, "Work Experience," should help you tremendously with this area.

In the following sections, I'm going to show you how to write better.

Writing Well

"How can you write well?"

Many people feel that their writing is not good. Even famous writers struggle with this feeling. And many people who need to put together a resume don't do much writing and have had little practice. At the same time, however, most people are good at telling a story to a friend — perhaps a funny thing that happened at the market, or an interesting program they saw on television. This ability is all you need to write a good resume! Your resume is really just a story about you.

You start with good content. If you are a poor worker and have accomplished little, your resume will not be impressive. But the fact that you are reading this book means that you are dedicated to improving your situation, and that's a sign of a good worker. If you have been reading and working with all the sections in Chapter 9, you have some good content by now. Now let's make it work for you.

I have identified ten principles of good writing. They are neither hard nor complicated to learn and follow, and they work. Apply them yourself and see!

First Principle: Use plain words.

The purpose of a resume is to impress the reviewer with your qualifications for the job. Many people think fancy writing is impressive. There are three problems with this. One, such writing is usually a turn-off. (Are you impressed by someone who uses a lot of flowery words? Or do you just think he or she is pompous?) Two, your resume should demonstrate how impressive YOU are — not your resume. Three, if you use boastful words incorrectly, not only do you fail to seem impressive; you seem downright dumb.

Look again at Example 3. You get the sense that the accomplishment is truly impressive. Yet the language is simple. Consider, for example, the phrase, "the first free democracy on earth." It contains no boastful words at all, but it says so much. Look at "negotiated the liberties of the people with the greatest minds of our time." It's an awesome accomplishment, but it uses words you learned in the third grade.

Here's an example of some overblown writing:

> My current employment situation encompasses the deployment of a duly licensed motorized vehicular conveyance in furtherance of conducting various personnel via local service routes from their place of location to their intended destinations.

This atrocious sentence means: I drive a taxi.

Here's a simple way to test whether your resume contains any bad overblown writing. Read it aloud to a friend. Can you keep a straight face? Or are you embarrassed?

Here's another example of unnecessarily pompous writing:

> I exercise full authority and unilaterally make major decisions and commitments of a binding nature in all areas related to the IRM program.

This sentence means: Hold authority for major decisions and commitments in all areas of the IRM program.

One more example of unnecessarily complex writing:

> Incorporating the technologies of GroupWare, Electronic Mail, File Sharing and RDBMS in an effort complicated by the lack of established operational functions, procedures and requirements for the NPFC to comply with its mandate, as stated in the Oil Pollution Act of 1990, of establishing systems to manage the Oil Spill Liability Trust Fund.

After an application of "plain language": Without established operational functions, incorporated the technologies of GroupWare, Electronic Mail, and File Sharing to manage the Oil Spill Liabilities Trust Fund information. Ensured compliance with the Oil Pollution Act of 1990.

Plain language is the single most important key to good resume writing. But if your resume does not pass the "straight face" test, how do you go about making it simple?

You must look critically at EVERY SINGLE WORD in your resume. Every word must pull its weight. You must mercilessly chop out every word that does not pack a punch. Use the fewest words possible to say the most.

I cannot stress this enough. You must literally consider every single word and phrase to determine whether it adds real meaning and substance to the sentence.

Exercise

Try this analysis on your own. Take the wordy writing sample below and make it simple. Use the fewest possible words. Then read it aloud. Does it sound natural? If so, you are on the right track. A suggested re-write is provided at the end of the chapter.

> I am presently engaged in the process of employing multitudinous units of verbiage to enhance the lucidity of the premise, with elaboration thereon, regarding the utility of the disencumbering of written materials which are afflicted with excessive circumlocution.

 Tip | If you can't read your resume aloud with a straight face, change it.

Second Principle: Use short sentences.

Long sentences are confusing and boring. They do not belong in your resume. Short sentences crackle with excitement! Abraham Lincoln once made the statement, "If you need me to give a long speech, I am ready now. If you want me to give a short speech, it will take me some time to prepare." No wonder the Gettysburg Address consists of just ten short sentences. What is true of speeches is even truer of resumes. The last thing you need in your resume is a string of long sentences that take the reviewer a lot of time and effort to figure out.

It is actually faster and easier to write long, complex sentences. Cutting them down to the essentials is an extra step, requiring more time and thought. It is critical that you make the extra effort to trim your sentences down to the real meat. I doubt that anyone has written a really good resume in the first draft. A resume is a very special form of writing that must be much more compact and concentrated than other types of documents. To get the kind of super-condensed sentences you need, you have to go through several drafts. Who's counting? It's infinitely better to take six drafts to boil it down to its most concise form than to submit a rambling first draft. The reviewer can't tell how many drafts it took you to get to the final product, but he or she can definitely tell if that final product is laden with unnecessary words.

Tip Ideally, a sentence conveys only one clear thought.

Ideally, a sentence conveys only one clear thought. It flows logically from the preceding sentence, and leads into the next sentence. There is no magically prescribed length for a good sentence, and good writing generally alternates between sentences of medium length and sentences that are much shorter. This creates variety and can set up a rhythm that keeps the reader's attention. See?

For example, you may find that your sentences have grown too long. If so, you can break them into smaller sentences. Each small sentence can convey one piece of the full thought.

If you absolutely must resort to a longer sentence, at least use some punctuation to break it into comprehensible phrases.

* Commas separate distinct thoughts but all add up to the same sentence.

* Semicolons (;) separate thoughts, each thought can stand alone.

* Full colons (:) a list of items.

Some examples follow.

Too many ideas

BEFORE:

I established a new time management protocol enabling staff to improve their productivity which also increased morale.

AFTER:

I established a new time management protocol which enabled staff to improve their productivity, and which also increased morale.

Illogical flow of duties

BEFORE:

Evaluates applications; rates and ranks applicants, screen applications for a variety of occupations for minimum qualifications; provides advice on the various personnel programs available; provides technical support of staffing administrative services for a variety of lower graded clerical and/or special projects and prepares certificate of eligibles.

AFTER

Screen specialized occupational applications for minimum qualifications. Evaluate, rate and rank qualified applicants; prepare certificate of eligibles. Advise managers on personnel programs. Give technical support to lower graded staff. Coordinate special projects.

Too much for one sentence

BEFORE :

Coordinated review of specification, acquisition, statement of work, test plans and procedures documents, to ensure that all written test processes are in accordance with the Acquisition Management System (AMS), Test and Evaluation guidelines and WJHTC System Test and Evaluation Process documents.

AFTER

Coordinated review of all written test processes. Ensured compliance with Acquisition Management System (AMS), Test and Evaluation guidelines and WJHTC System Test and Evaluation Process documents. Reviewed specification, acquisition, statement of work, test plans and procedures documents.

The laundry list

BEFORE:

Direct the administration and management of a comprehensive support service program including visual information, naval messages, records, directives, forms and reports, mail operations, building management, graphics, command history, command mission and functions statements, military manning, printing and distribution, classified information, personnel security and military personnel programs.

AFTER:

Wrote, edited, and archived written communications, including: command mission and functions statements, messages, directives, forms and reports, printing and distribution, and classified information.

Managed operations including: facility management, mail operations, graphics coordination, military manning, personnel security and military personnel programs.

Communicated and directed military manning, personnel security, and military personnel and command mission.

 Tip In resumes, less truly is more. You are not paid by the word. Short, well-constructed sentences, packed with meaningful content, are far superior to long sentences.

Third Principle: Limit the use of "I."

There is no *I* in *resume*. Avoid writing your resume with the personal pronoun "I." Resumes are a unique breed of writing in which sentence fragments are preferred, as long as their meaning is clear. Omit the first person pronoun and most other pronouns and articles whenever possible. The before and after examples below demonstrate the replacement of a strong verb instead of "I am responsible for, I performed, I am the ..." Your resume will become a more active document when you replace the "I" with a solid verb.

BEFORE:

I am responsible for the Strategic Information Resources Management (IRM) Plan, all automated system projects from formulation through implementation to include the development of "Automated Information Systems Proposals," the annual funding plan, and the allocation of funding among all the IRM projects.

AFTER:

Manage the implementation of the first Strategic Information Resources Management Plan, as well as all automated system projects. Direct projects from formulation through implementation. Coordinate development of "Automated Information Systems Proposals," the annual funding plan, and the allocation of funding among all the IRM projects.

BEFORE:

I performed a multitude of administrative functions, such as preparing for Command Inspections, assuming responsibility for office functions in the temporary absence of Directors, scheduling conference room functions, advising staff members of recommended policies and established procedures

AFTER:

Planned and prepared for Command Inspections representing the Directors in their absence. Advised staff members of inspection policies and procedures; scheduled the conference room and meetings; coordinated efficient logistics.

BEFORE:

I am the principal technical expert dedicated to the functions of planning, developing, implementing, and evaluating the Information Resources Management (IRM) program for the overall Reserve Training Program.

AFTER:

Principal technical expert for the overall Reserve Training Program, Information Resources Management. Direct the development, implementation, and evaluation of the effectiveness of the Reserve training program.

BEFORE:

I typed a wide variety of materials, using various software (i.e., correspondence, personnel forms, charts, instructions/directives, reports, proposals, and recommendations related to studies) from drafts or dictation. I was responsible for establishing and maintaining files to facilitate the storage and retrieval of pertinent information, including management studies and civilian personnel administration.

AFTER:

Word processed in Word 7.0 and WordPerfect correspondence, instructions, directives and proposals in support of training programs. Designed an archive system for management studies and civilian personnel actions.

	Info	In some of the samples of good resume writing in this chapter, you will see the word "I." This is because the sample, which has no context, would have been unclear without "I." In your resume, the context may make the meaning clear, and you can safely delete the "I."

Fourth Principle: Use powerful words.

If you use plain language in short sentences, how is your resume going to impress anyone? Through the use of powerful words! In Example 3, I used *principal architect* to describe James Madison's role as the main drafter of the Constitution. *Main* becomes *principal. Drafter* is boring. *Architect* indicates an active process by a trained professional with a tangible result.

Powerful words are words that convey strong and unambiguous meaning. You should use a thesaurus to find stronger substitutes for weak words in your resume. But this won't take you all the way. To clear away the debris of weak words, you need to think about writing in a new way. For example, consider the following statement:

Serve as point of contact for all matters pertaining to personnel.

Serve as is not impressive. It does not tell you anything. Chop it. *Point of contact* is good, but *chief liaison* is better. *Sole liaison* is better still (if true). *Pertaining to* adds nothing, so eliminate it. Just say, *all personnel matters.* Thus, the following statement is a good phrase:

Sole liaison on all personnel matters.

Every single word in it contributes significantly to the idea. Can you cut any word out of your resume and not lose some meaningful bit of information?

To get more power out of words, convert verbose phrases into economical nouns. *Tasks include administrative aspects of office management* becomes *Office manager* or *Administrator of 25 staff office.* Remember the chapter on *Hats, Nouns and Verbs*? Include more nouns in your resume wherever you can.

Powerful Words for Resume Writing

The following list is a compilation of more than 100 powerful words for resume writing. There are undoubtedly many more. This list is based on more than 15 years experience at professional writing. I suggest that you make a copy of the list and post it near your computer or wherever you work on your resume as a handy reference. It will be a great tool when you are stuck for a word. It is arranged into categories. Just by picking words from the various categories and modifying them as needed, you will already be halfway to a quality resume.

These words are nouns and verbs, quantifiers, interpersonal traits, abilities, core competencies, and industry jargon. These exceptional words will demonstrate your level of independence and impress the reader.

Creation

These verbs demonstrate initiative, resourcefulness, organizational skills, and creativity.

assemble	conceive	convene	create
design	effectively	forge	form
formulate	implement	initiate	invent
plan	realize	spearhead	

First or Only

The Navy Job Kit gives these instructions "Use modifiers to define the frequency at which you perform tasks, i.e., occasionally, regularly, once or twice per year, monthly, weekly, daily. Use words that define the level and scope of your experience and skills." These quantifiers are important. If you do not tell readers you were the sole support for 15 professionals, how will they know it?

chief	first	foremost	greatest
leading	most	number one	one
only	prime	single	singular
sole	top	unique	unparalleled
unrivaled			

Outcomes

To demonstrate that you can "get things done," use these words to demonstrate action and results.

communication	cooperation	cost-effective	efficiency
morale	outcomes	output	productivity

Deployment

These words demonstrate movement, action, and decision-making capabilities.

deploy	employ	exercise	use
utilize			

Leadership

Leaders are in demand — whether you are a manager, administrative staff, or in the trades. If you are a team leader, foreman, supervisor, or lead, define your leadership responsibilities.

(be) chief (of)
(be) in charge of
(be) responsible for

administer	control	direct	govern
head	head up	lead	manage
oversee	run	supervise	

Primacy

How important are you to the project? Are you a subject matter expert? If you are, say so.

advisor	co-worker	key	major
primary	principal	subject matter	expert
lead	source person	sole source	

Persuasion

The ability to persuade is a significant trait for anyone. Persuasive skills and language can be used in describing teamwork.

coach	galvanize	inspire	lobby
persuade	rally	unify	unite
(re)invigorate	(re)vitalize		

Success

The word "success" suggests results and positive thinking. The reader believes that you are successful because you have written it in your resume.

accomplish	achieve	attain	master
score (a victory)	succeed	sustain	

Authorship

Writing is one of the principal skills needed in a civilian's job. If you write and edit documents, please include these skills.

author	create	draft	generate
write	managing editor	editor	publish

Newness

Are you part of a project that is being done for the first time? Tell readers or they won't know this is an innovative, state-of-the-art program designed to improve services and enhance the program.

creative	first-ever	first-of-its-kind	innovative
novel	state-of-the-art		

Degree

Quantify your successes and results — with a percentage, if possible. Your resume will be more interesting, complete and exciting.

100% (or other percent that is impressive)

completely	considerably	effectively	especially
extremely	fully	greatly	highly
outstanding	particularly	powerful	seasoned
significantly	solidly	strongly	thoroughly
veteran			

Quality

Qualify your work efforts. Was it excellent, outstanding, high quality? Positive thinking and writing about outstanding achievements will sell the selecting official on your capabilities.

excellent	good	great	high quality
outstanding quality	special	superb	

Competencies

Writing about your knowledge, skills, and abilities in your resume requires that you state you are adept in concise, focused writing; expert in certain laws and regulations; capable in facilitating meetings; and skilled in Network administration.

able	adept at	capable	competent
demonstrated	effective	expert	knowledgeable
proven	skilled	tested	trained
versed in			

Words to Edit Out of Your Resume

Just as there are powerful words that serve you well in a resume, there are some words and phrases to avoid. Here are a few "before" and "after" examples of the old writing style and the new, more succinct writing style.

Currently I am working as the Manager of Operations
Manage operations

I also have experience with planning meetings
Plan and coordinate meetings

I have worked for the Office of Training Programs Cooperate with Office of Training Programs

I have helped set up office systems
Organized new office systems

Major duties include working with other staff
Cooperated with staff

I used a variety of equipment
Equipment skills include:

Major duties were to write and edit
Write and edit …

I provide… Select a verb that will be more descriptive than "provide," such as design, research, coordinate, facilitate.

Worked in the capacity of management analyst
Management Analyst

I was responsible for managing the daily operations
Managed daily operations

I also have experience in designing audit reports
Design audit reports

When needed, supervise team members
Supervise team members on occasion

As the Department's user support
User support for the Department

Worked with team members
Member of a team

Being the timekeeper for the office
Timekeeper for the office

Assume duties of the education specialist
Education specialist planing programs and curriculum

Also responsible for preparing payroll information

Prepare payroll for 250 employees

Have the authority to Cooperate with
authors and editors in the publication of

Helped with writing, editing
Wrote, edited, planned, coordinated ... any verb that describes the activity.

Tasks included compiling, organizing and researching information
Compile, organize and research information

Assisted with planning, researching, and designing
Co-planned, researched, and designed the

As a member of a team, planned, researched and designed
Planned, researched and designed as a member of the interagency team

Responsible for all aspects of critical reviews and narrative reports for
Wrote critical reviews and narrative reports for

I provide the leadership to maintain benchmarks to meet project deadlines.
Plan and lead team to maintain benchmarks to meet project deadlines.

Concurrently monitored project ...
Managed project details for the _____ project

My other duties consist of customer services, research and problem-solving
Research and resolve problems for customers.

I also design and write technical guidebooks
Write and design technical guidebooks.

The above information is gathered from various
Compiled, organized and managed information gathered from

I have to do systems analysis and planning
Manage systems analysis and planning for projects

Assisted in all aspects of
Involved in all aspects of

Those are just some of the phrases to avoid, because there are stronger ways to express yourself. The key is to review every single word and phrase in your resume. Then ask yourself two questions:

1. If I cut it out, would the sentence be less meaningful?

2. Is there any shorter or clearer way to say it?

If you can honestly answer no to both questions, leave it in. I look at it this way: you have to work hard; so should each word in your resume!

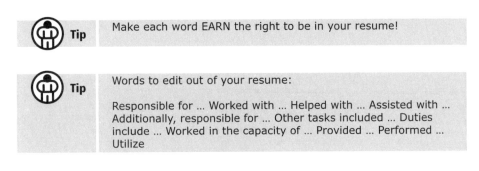

Tip Make each word EARN the right to be in your resume!

Tip Words to edit out of your resume:

Responsible for … Worked with … Helped with … Assisted with … Additionally, responsible for … Other tasks included … Duties include … Worked in the capacity of … Provided … Performed … Utilize

Fifth Principle: Beware of acronyms.

There are several reasons why you should not depend on acronyms to describe your job.

1. Many people may not recognize your acronyms. Your direct supervisor may understand perfectly, but readers outside your specific agency and office may not know your specific terminology. You are attempting to write "One Resume Fits All," so the acronyms should be considered carefully.

2. The general grammar in the database may not contain your acronyms. The local grammar produced by your human resources office may or may not have all of your acronyms in the database. Describe your experience with both acronyms and description to be safe.

If you ask someone to read your paragraph aloud and it is filled with acronyms, it will be difficult to understand.

Here are "before" and "after" job descriptions for two positions, a Personnel Assistant and an Oceanographer.

Personnel Assistant

BEFORE:

Amended/cancelled/deleted from OPM and DASN vacancy Web sites and other types of creative recruitment techniques. Created DEU casefiles and maintained open, closed, pending, audit and current inventory according to OPM guidelines and regulations. Checked DAIWA, ACWA, and TDP requirements, downloading current qualification standards and generating announcement numbers and dates. I received and reviewed incoming SF-52's before certificates were released.

AFTER:

Managed and performed quality checks on vacancy announcements posted on Office of Personnel Management (OPM) and Navy Web sites. Amended and updated the announcements and determined other creative recruitment techniques. Researched current qualification standards and produced new announcements. Opened external recruitment case files and managed applicant inventory based on personnel guidelines. Reviewed applicant minimum qualifications and certifications and documents, including personnel actions (SF-51s) and Request for Referral (SF-39s). Reviewed the list of Interagency Placement Program requests (IPP). Prepared the Certificates for qualified candidates for selecting officials.

Oceanographer

BEFORE:

Advocate for the Oceanographer of the Navy's programs during several of these meetings. Developed a comprehensive outline and criteria for validating representations of the real-world battlespace environment and the representations of the real-world METOC and terrain decision aid information processing systems for JSIMS. Developed a "METOC Support CONOPS for JSIMS" incorporating the Navy's METOC concept of operations.

AFTER:

Advocate for the Oceanographer of the Navy's programs during several of these meetings. Developed a comprehensive outline and criteria for validating representations of the real-world battlespace environment and the meteorological, oceanographic and terrain decision aid information processing systems. Emphasized the importance of including the effects of battlespace environment phenomena, such as including effects of shallow water on acoustic energy propagation, surf conditions on amphibious raids/assaults, and radar ducting conditions on target acquisitions.

 Tip Limit your use of acronyms in your resume. Write the acronym if you are repeating it later in the paragraph, or if the acronym is common.

Sixth Principle: No bureaucratese, colloquialisms, or technobabble.

You will recognize some of the bureaucratese writing style when you begin to rewrite your content from your application forms into the new resume. Here's a definition of bureaucratese: *A style of language characterized by jargon and euphemism that is used especially by bureaucrats.*

Bureaucratese?

This is the language bureaucrats speak, and it is often a confusing, cold and cloudy one. All of us, but particularly those of us who work for the public, have a responsibility to handle the language with care. We need to be accessible and clear. We need to avoid jargon and bureaucratese. Examples include:

* Overuse of the passive voice

* Using federal and state program names without explaining what the programs are

* Using and misusing words like impact, interface, prioritize, modality, and ascertain

* Using phony words like analyzation, conduit, augment, determine the nature of, etc...

Resume writing is a challenge for the federal employee who is stuck in the mindset of the long, bureaucratic writing style of the SF-171. Every sentence typically begins with: "Responsible for ..." or "Other responsibilities include ..." Start breaking those old habits now. This entire chapter is dedicated to breaking you from this "official-sounding" writing style habit!

Colloquialisms?

Do I even have to say it? Resumes simply cannot be colloquial, chatty, cute, clever, or otherwise casual — especially in the civilian DOD agency environment. They must be purely professional. This does not mean that they should be stiff or overly formal — just professional. Where do you draw the line? You must know the audience. If you are applying for a position in finance or other fields demanding precision and accountability, casual language may easily disqualify you. If your goal is a job doing puppet shows for children in hospitals, some flexibility in the direction of the casual may not hurt. The bottom line: better to be too professional than too colloquial, no matter what the position.

Technobabble?

Computer professionals are a good example of resume writers who typically write either too much or too little. Either way, it is a challenge to get a full, clear sentence that a non-technical person can understand. An Information Technology (IT) professional in today's working world, must be able to communicate verbally and in writing with customers who are struggling to use information technology systems efficiently.

I met an IT entrepreneur on an airplane who told me that he never hires a computer person who does not include the word "customer" in his or her resume. In fact, he says he hires IT professionals for their ability to communicate and provide customer service. The technical skills are expected, but the service side is the real challenge. In your resume, I would recommend that you consider technical expertise and communications skills equally. Remember who is reading the resume: human resources, customers, administrators, and technology managers. The complex, long, multiple-thought sentences won't impress readers if they can't understand the meaning.

Here's a "before" and "after" excerpt of a technical description.

BEFORE:

Identified operational program problems and issues and conducted analysis to determine the nature of requirements, logical work and information flows to ascertain the type of Information Processing technology required to support the Reserve Training Program.

AFTER:

Recommended Information Processing technology systems for the Reserve Training program. Identified operational program problems and analyzed information and workflow.

Seventh Principle: Tell a story. Describe a project.

The best resumes flow with well-written, interesting prose — almost like a story. Many Federal employees are involved in major projects in their work. Their entire resume can be composed of descriptions of projects. The section in Chapter 9 entitled *What Have You Accomplished Lately?* includes examples of accomplishments and projects that can make your resume interesting and demonstrate specific knowledge, skills, and abilities.

On a resume, you can tell a story this way:

Director: Special Backlog Reduction Project, May-June, 2000

Appointed by Office Manager to lead special project to reduce chronic filing backlog. Devised innovative cross-reference filing system that significantly reduced file retrieval time. Reported to work one hour early each day for one month to remedy backlog, while still performing all regular duties. Successfully eliminated 13-month backlog within 30 days. Office Manager commended me in writing for this achievement, and mandated adoption of my new system department-wide.

This story shows that you are hard working and conscientious, punctual (even coming in one hour early), organized, and more — all of the qualities you wanted to convey. I also gave you a special title for this position. The title sounds important and says exactly what you did. You can use such a title to good effect, even if the Office Manager never officially bestowed it, as long as it is true. Speaking of which....

Eighth Principle: Tell the truth and don't exaggerate.

An attorney once served on a committee to assess the qualifications of applicants for an elite unit. Each applicant submitted a resume and a writing sample. As he was reading one of the writing samples, it struck him as being well written, but familiar. This is no surprise, since the attorney had written it! The applicant had plagiarized his work for her writing sample (probably not realizing this person would be reviewing it). Needless to say, this individual did not get the job.

The greatest writing in the world is worth nothing if the content is not true. This goes not only for blatant plagiarism, but for undue exaggeration. We all want to put the best spin on our qualifications in our resumes. That's the point of a resume. But if you exaggerate your accomplishments to the extent of being misleading, you are hurting yourself.

In the same category, avoid superlatives as a general rule. Phrases such as "all," "very," "every," "the greatest," "the only," etc., raise a red flag. Don't say that you scored the highest performance rating on a particular task ever recorded in the history of the agency, unless it is literally true. On the other hand, when the accomplishment is literally true, superlatives are pretty impressive.

Use superlatives only for objectively quantifiable accomplishments. Like this:

> Prepared 18 consecutive budgets; was never late, and every budget was adopted after full review without change.

Do not use superlatives for subjective assessments. It is meaningless to say, "I am the most efficient office manager ever." According to what scale? The one exception is when reciting the opinion of a knowledgeable person. "My supervisor has praised me as being the most efficient office manager he has ever known." Though subjective, the opinion of a supervisor is meaningful.

Ninth Principle: Be consistent with your verb tenses.

The rule about tense in resumes is to use the present tense for all present responsibilities and skills and the past tense for all past responsibilities. Here are a few samples:

DEPUTY TEAM LEADER, LITIGATION TEAM (January, 1999 to present)

Trusted assistant and advisor to Team Leader. Authorized to make executive-level decisions, such as approving settlements in cases handled by staff attorneys. Currently sole attorney in charge of three of the five most significant cases in Department (as assessed by Senior Partner). *(Present tense)*

ELECTRONICS TECHNICIAN (September, 1990 to present)

Field installer. Ensure the security and protection of the University property and individuals through electronic systems. Install, test, maintain, and repair electronic security systems throughout the campus. Troubleshoot systems and communicate with contractors concerning warranty and specialized repairs. (*Present tense*)

SENIOR STAFF ATTORNEY (August, 1997 to December, 1998)

Handled over 75 complex litigations from start to finish. Promoted from Attorney Level II to Attorney Level III in record time. Carried caseload 42% above office-wide average. Consistently rated "outstanding," highest possible rating. Won annual award for "Top-Performing Staff Attorney" three years in a row. *(Past tense.)*

Use the active voice whenever possible. Meaning, that your sentence has a subject and a verb, and the subject is performing the action indicated by the verb. For example: *I handled over 75 complex litigations.* "I" is the subject. "*Handled*" is the verb. For resume writing, in order to not start every sentence with "I," the subject is assumed. Therefore, the sentence is written: Handled over 75 complex litigations. All of the sentences above could start with "I," but we have deleted "I" so that the sentences emphasize the action, rather than the subject.

Tenth Principle: Avoid the passive voice.

Human resources professionals write vacancy announcements in the passive voice. Many civilians became accustomed to writing their SF-171s in the passive voice. Avoid using the passive voice. The opposite of the active voice is the passive voice. A sentence in the passive voice has a subject and a verb, but the subject is not doing the action of the verb. Rather, the subject is having the action of the verb done to it by someone or something else. For example: *The sentence is being written.* "Sentence" is the subject. "To write" is the verb, but it is no longer active. The sentence is not writing. Someone else is writing. Who? We don't know. The passive voice is vague and elusive because it raises a question (who is writing?) but does not supply an answer, which is annoying.

Identifying passive sentences is sometimes confusing in resumes because the subject is often "I," and is often omitted from the sentence.

Here are a few examples of passive voice followed by the active voice. The passive voice examples don't say that the person really DID anything. Someone else did the work, or the statement is simply a statement without action.

Information Technology Professional

BEFORE

Other duties: classroom control (25 to 30 students in each class), student discipline, and student grading and evaluations — much the same as a supervisor but with more bodies. Work entails handling multiple tasks in the classroom; flexibility, discipline, alertness a requirement in this job. Must also be a good listener at all times.

AFTER:

Managed classroom control (25 to 30 students in each class), student discipline, and student grading and evaluations. Demonstrated classroom flexibility, discipline, listening skills, and alertness in meeting student needs.

Property Management Specialist

BEFORE:

When the property management program began coordinating the property acquisition, job responsibilities were aligned more closely with the procurement process. This job assisted offices in acquiring necessary equipment and services. The Data Systems Division continued to improve and enhance the property management application.

AFTER:

Established a property management program for the Data Systems Division. Procured equipment and services and advised staff in purchasing processes.

Computer Programmer Analyst

BEFORE:

Responsible for developing automated systems for administrative and investigative functions. While most applications were hosted by the mainframe, several projects involved "downsizing" applications to the PC.

AFTER:

Designed mainframe and PC automated systems for administrative and investigative functions.

Associate Director of Nursing

BEFORE:

Provided administrative oversight to the Housekeeping Department, Hospital Infection Control Program, and Human Resources Department.

AFTER:

Directed the Housekeeping and Human Resources Departments and the Hospital Infection Control Program.

Senior Supervisory Program Management Officer, GS-13

BEFORE:

Responsible for planning, implementing and directing all aspects of health services delivery to a population of approximately 1,100 Federal inmates. Provided administrative supervision over a staff of 22, including 13 Physician's Assistants, 2 Physicians, 2 Dentists, 1 pharmacist and four support personnel. Had fiscal responsibility for preparation of the budget as well as expenditure of appropriated funds, procurement, and formulation of BoP policy. Responsible for the establishment and maintenance of a Quality Management Program to ensure program.

AFTER:

Planned and directed health services delivery to approximately 1,100 Federal inmates. Supervised a staff of 22, including 13 Physician's Assistants, 2 Physicians, 2 Dentists, 1 pharmacist, and 4 support personnel. Managed the budget, as well as expenditure of appropriated funds, procurement, and formulation of policy. Established and maintained a Quality Management Program.

To eliminate the passive voice from your resume, simply identify the subject of each sentence and verify that the subject is performing the action indicated by the verb. If you find a passive sentence and you cannot figure out a way to convert it to a natural-sounding active sentence, try selecting a different verb. If this doesn't work, try using a different subject. If neither works, throw the sentence out. If you can't say it actively, it doesn't belong in your resume.

And finally: Be yourself.

Since your resume reflects who you are, you should feel comfortable with it. Can you speak it out loud without embarrassment? If not, you could end up being embarrassed if the interviewer asks you about your accomplishments as recorded on the resume.

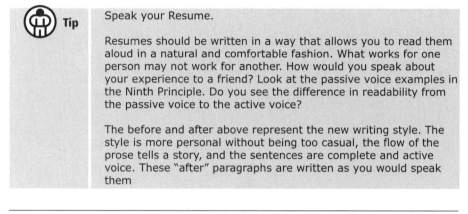

Tip   Speak your Resume.

Resumes should be written in a way that allows you to read them aloud in a natural and comfortable fashion. What works for one person may not work for another. How would you speak about your experience to a friend? Look at the passive voice examples in the Ninth Principle. Do you see the difference in readability from the passive voice to the active voice?

The before and after above represent the new writing style. The style is more personal without being too casual, the flow of the prose tells a story, and the sentences are complete and active voice. These "after" paragraphs are written as you would speak them

Chapter Review

Which brings us back to that question, **How do you look on paper?**

You want your resume to be impressive. You realize that your resume, no matter how artfully drafted, can only be truly impressive if you are confident in your capabilities and experience.

I enjoy writing resumes for people, mainly because I delight in helping people see that their innate worth can be made into a powerful resume. You can do this for yourself. Are you conscientious, intelligent, and hard working? Then you deserve full credit for these virtues! Rejoice in your strengths; identify your many unsung achievements; and put them on paper in plain language. I guarantee that your resume will be honest and impressive — just like you!

Lastly, I promised you a re-write of a horrible sentence I perpetrated earlier in the "Exercise." Did you figure out what it meant? Here it is, rewritten:

> I am using far too many words in this sentence to show you the importance of freeing your writing from too many words.

Chapter 12

Electronic Resumes — Dos and Don'ts

Follow the job kit instructions.
Follow the vacancy announcement instructions.

Think about your audience. Electronic resumes have two readers: the computer system that will read the resume for key words; and the hiring manager who will read the resume to select the best candidate. The readability of your resume by both reviewers is important for your candidacy, so follow these tips.

Consider the process. You will have to learn new directions and systems with the electronic automated process. Once you learn the process, the job search and selection process is faster and better. Be patient and follow the new HR trends.

Do

Prepare

* Research keywords, skills, and industry language.

* Locate all of your written career papers, such as resumes, 171s, position descriptions.

* Schedule time to research, write, and edit.

* Consider this a career management project, not a resume.

* Focus your skills and career interests — this is critical!

* Find an editor and second reader to review your draft.

Resume Writing

* Write one resume that will focus on all of your career objectives.

* Research and include key skills in your electronic resume.

* Follow the page length instructions in each job kit.

* If you are writing a 5-page resume, write your most important information within the first 3 pages. The 199 skills bucket

could fill up by 3 pages. This is described in more detail in Chapter 2.

* If a Resume Builder asks for a specific section for which you have no experience (for example, Certifications, Awards or Training), it's okay to leave them blank.

* Be specific when naming the computer software or types of equipment and tools with which you have experience.

* Describe your experience using specific words rather than vague generalizations.

* Complete supplemental and additional data sheets thoroughly. The answers to these questions are very important during recruiter searches.

* Be selective with acronyms. Spell out acronyms when they are first written in the resume. If they are not needed further in the text, try to use words.

* Limit experience to recent jobs and jobs that directly support your qualifications.

* Summarize several jobs that are the same into one job. You may have different grades, different geographic locations, or different supervisors, but if the job is basically the same, describe it as *one* job. If you are a Management Analyst and you were hired in 1990 as a GS-7 and now you're a GS-11 working in the same office, this is one job. Write the description of this job at the highest level and list the current supervisor.

* Write the name of your current organization. If the organization has changed names several times, just use the last/current name.

* Include substantial unpaid job experience as a job block.

Electronic Resume Type Fonts

* Use one of the following typefaces: Helvetica, Futura, Optima, Universe, Times, Palatino, New Century Schoolbook, and Courier.

* Use the preferred font size: 12 points. You must stay in the 11–14 point range.

* Make sure each page has a one-inch margin on all sides.

* Print your resume on white bond paper, one side only, using a laser jet printer, if you are submitting a paper resume by mail (not preferred, but acceptable in some regions).

* If you copy and paste your resume content into a Resume Builder, the typefont and paper requirements will be irrelevant.

Formatting and Readability

* Use ALL CAPS for highlighting job titles or other important items. Do not overuse all caps. See the samples on the CD-ROM for an effective use of all caps.

* Add white space for readability. Keep paragraph lengths at eight to ten lines maximum. Put a double space between paragraphs to improve readability and add white space.

* Follow the electronic resume formats on the CD-ROM. Copy and paste the text into as many resume builders as you can find time to submit.

Resume Builders

* If a resume builder tells you to put a hard return at the end of every line, don't do it. Just write with small paragraphs (5 to 10 lines). Put a hard return at the end of the paragraph.

* Most resume builders give you space for six jobs.

* Do not write your original resume in a resume builder.

* Write your resume in your favorite word processor in 12-point type, Times or Helvetica. Follow the formats on the CD-ROM for Work Experience details. This will give you an accurate page length.

* Copy and paste this text into the resume builders.

* Keep your passwords (VERY IMPORTANT).

Submit Your Resume

* The preferred method for your resume submission is through a resume builder. This way you can review and update your resume periodically.

* The second preferred method is through e-mail, usually copied and pasted into the text box of the e-mail.

* The third way to send your resume is through the mail in a large envelope, unstapled and flat. This is not a preferred method and in many cases will not be accepted.

Self-Nominate

* Read the vacancy announcements to determine if you should self-nominate for a position.

* Read the vacancy announcements to determine if the position is an *open continuously* or an *inventory-building announcement.* If so, submit your resume for unannounced vacancies.

* Self-nominate when you have already submitted your resume into a database.

* Keep track of your resume-builder submissions and self-nominations. Use the Database Log Sheet on the CD-ROM to record your submissions.

Update Your Resume

* Read the directions about updating, activating and special days to update.

* Update at least three days before an announcement closes.

* Update once per year or once every six months at least.

Don't

* Fill up your skills bucket with wasted names of systems, acronyms, and other unrelated words. (Remember the skills bucket from Chapter 2? The resume included unneeded words, included: *cooking, vinyl, recipe, restaurant* and all of her

courses. The preferred skills would have been administrative or project skills that would be relevant to her objective.)

* Follow the resume builder guidelines for maximum number of characters for all fields. The resume builder may have spaces for a total of 32,000 characters. If you fill up all the fields, it could end up with a 6- to 10-page resume. You will be rejected with that length.

* Be repetitive. The software will give you credit for words only one time. You will not get extra points for saying things more than one time.

* Use vertical or horizontal lines, graphics, or boxes.

* Use fancy fonts or typefaces.

* Submit your resume on colored paper.

* Use a two-column format.

* Use flowery prose. It wastes space that could be used for listing skills.

* Submit additional documentation unless requested.

* If you are mailing your resume, don't staple, fold, or punch holes in your resume.

* Write phrases like *Responsible for, Worked with, Helped with, Assisted with, Other tasks include, In addition.* DO write with verbs and nouns in the active voice. Please refer to Chapter 11 "Plain Language Resumes" to refresh your writing skills.

* Fax your electronic resume. Faxes tend to scan poorly.

* Attach your resume as an attachment to an e-mail. You should copy the resume and additional data sheet into the textbox. See an example of a resume in a textbox of an email in the CD-ROM. (Resume-builder submissions are preferred.)

Chapter Review

The important things to DO when writing a successful electronic resume are to plan, research keywords, write concisely, and then submit your resume correctly into as many resume builders and databases as you have interest in. The biggest differences between the electronic resume and the federal resume or a private industry resume is *format*. You will be writing a good, focused and easy-to-read resume for any resume format. The electronic resumes are plain in format. You can see samples of the electronic resumes on the CD-ROM. It is important that the computer system "read" your resume, but it is also important that the hiring manager can read your resume too.

What's Next?

The appendix of this book contains two electronic resume samples that follow the TO DO list above. I think you will be inspired to work on your new resume after seeing the final resumes. You'll also see a list of the Job Kits and Web sites for DOD agencies who are using the electronic resume. Decide which agency is of most interest to you and start reading those instructions. I recommend that you focus on one agency at a time.

The CD-ROM is a book in itself. The content of the CD-ROM includes excellent final samples of DOD civilian resumes at all grade levels, private industry samples (just in case), and techniques for researching keywords and industry terminology. After you study the keywords and skills buckets on the CD-ROM, you will be anxious to begin your own research for your skills list. You will never again depend on your position description for the best possible language to write your resume. You will be trained for original research for your own words to write the best possible electronic resume — a resume that will get hits resulting in notification that you've been found qualified and impress the selecting official. It's all up to you. Good luck with writing your electronic resume and playing the resume-builder game! It will work!

Info CARRIAGE RETURNS? Many job kit instructions state: "Use carriage returns after line/paragraph breaks." Here's the truth about the "hard returns": An Army Resumix Team Member writes: "Hard page breaks do not have to be put after every line, but our experience is that 'large' blocks of text sometimes cause problems with the e-mail functions. 'Occasional' hard breaks are recommended."

Tips Follow the "Golden Rule" of resume writing: compose your resume so that it can be read and understood by someone who has never worked in your area. In other words, get your neighbor or grandmother to read your resume. If he or she can understand it, you've written a good resume!

Tips Emphasize explanations of knowledge, skills, and abilities over long lists of system acronyms in your resume.

Info One resume-builder user filled in every job block totaling 11,096 characters — six pages. The Army Job Kit instructions stated three pages was the maximum length. He lost consideration for a couple of jobs because he couldn't edit and resubmit fast enough.

Appendixes

Appendix A: Sample Electronic Resumes

DIVISION SECRETARY, OFFICE AUTOMATION, GS-318-04 ADMINISTRATIVE ASSISTANT

PROGRAM ASSISTANT
MANAGEMENT ASSISTANT
PERSONNEL CLERK / PERSONNEL ASSISTANT

SUSAN L. GAINES

SSN: 000000000

10000 Pearl River Road

Pearl River, MS 39466

Home Phone: 228 688-4886

Work Phone: 601 798-4294

E-Mail Address: SusanLGaines@aol.com

WORK EXPERIENCE

Job 1

08/1996 to present; 40 hours per week.

DIVISION SECRETARY, OFFICE AUTOMATION, GS-318-04, $24,800 annually.

Naval Oceanography Office, Warfighting Support Center, Special Projects Division, N23, 1002 Balch Blvd., Stennis Space Center, MS 39522-5001.

Supervisor: T. Thomas Wizard, Phone: 228-688-4444. Permission to contact.

Plan and delegate administrative tasks to staff. Work independently. Utilize office automation, financial, and logistics software programs. Handle all correspondence sent from N23. Compose, review, proofread and ensure accurate spelling, organization, grammar, punctuation, and formatting. Type reports, letters, Memoranda of Agreement and NAVOCEANO Instructions. Member of NAVOCEANO Correspondence Process Action Team, PAT; develop strategies for improving all aspects of NAVOCEANO correspondence.

Provide information support and assure timely processing of personnel and payroll actions for 50 Division employees, including health insurance, retirement, leave, awards, worker's compensation, and related personnel and payroll actions. Write position descriptions.

Annually handle 1,000 to 1,500 RFPs for the Warfighting Support Center; perform database updates, create reports, and monitor RFPs. Interface with Commanding Officer, Technical Director, Executive Officer, and Department Heads. Apply knowledge of Privacy Act and Freedom of Information Act.

MENTOR AND COACH—Taught division secretaries in office automation, setting up filing systems, and NAVOCEANO organizational policies and procedures. Assisted and encourage deaf employee in pursuing career opportunities; facilitate reasonable accommodations.

ACCOMPLISHMENTS: 1999 Selected for NAVOCEANO's Long-Term Training program and attended college full-time, with all expenses paid. Rated Outstanding for performance and recognized for assumption of additional duties.

Job 2

05/2000 to 08/2000; 40 hours per week.

DIVISION SECRETARY, OFFICE AUTOMATION, GS-318-04

Customer Service Division. 90-day detail assignment as ADMINISTRATIVE ASSISTANT. Received Requests for Products, RFPs, from military and civilian customers; coordinated with appropriate code for production; data process requests into database; ran queries on customer base and product types. Monitored Web updates to ensure newest products are posted. Coordinated with producers to update product lists. Ran metrics for weekly briefs and command status input. Updated database for briefings to top managers. Disseminated all products produced in division and notified quality control and Security personnel to ensure accuracy of product before mailing or posting. Followed up with customers to obtain opinions on quality of products.

Job 3

10/1993 to 07/1997; 40 hours per week.

DIVISION SECRETARY, OFFICE AUTOMATION, GS-318-04, $21,000 annually.

Naval Oceanography Office, Warfighting Support Center, Satellite Analysis Division N21, 1002 Balch Blvd., Stennis Space Center, MS 39522-5001.

Supervisor: Thomas L. Smith, Phone: 228-688-4444.

Supported Branch by producing correspondence, reports, forms, and other documents. Maintained timecards, correspondence filing system, office calendar, office supplies and equipment, received and referred callers and visitors, arranged appointments, distribute mail log classified material, handled travel itineraries and prepared travel vouchers. Arranged meetings and conferences. Prepared all briefing slides for Commander. Designed and established a database using Lotus spread sheets for office budget and tracking purpose.

Job 4

02/1992 to 06/1993; 40 hours per week.

BRANCH SECRETARY, OFFICE AUTOMATION, GS-318-04, $16,400 annually.

NAVOCEANO, Operations Department, Special Products Branch, OWM, Stennis Space Center, MS 39522-5001 Supervisor: Blake Dowling, Retired

Supported Branch by producing correspondence, reports, forms, and other documents. Maintained time cards, correspondence filing system. Maintained classified filing system, office calendar, office supplies and equipment. Received and referred callers and visitors, arranged appointments, distributed mail log classified material, handled travel itineraries and prepared travel vouchers. Arranged meetings and conferences. Kept ship scheduler, acquisition plan for ship equipment, shipment of equipment. Liaison between office ship crew members and family.

Job 5

01/1993 to Present; 20 hours per week.

FINANCIAL MANAGER AND CO-OWNER, $30,000 annually.

P. A. Gaines Construction Company, Slidell, LA. Phone: 504 777-4110.

Customer and contractor dealings on all business aspects. Assess, recommend and present various options to customers; present written proposal on terms of contract and estimated costs. Design houses, utilizing Gantt charts for projects, oversee construction, quality control and control costs. Utilize Quick Pro 2000 for payroll, checking, monthly profit and loss statements, worker's compensation, listings of vendors, customers and employees, inventory of materials, W-2s and 1099 forms, and 1040 Federal Income Tax return. Crew work cutting and hanging vinyl siding. Design, plans, and perform cost analyses and manage all aspects of completed rental units.

ACCOMPLISHMENTS: Organized and established comprehensive office management and bookkeeping system. Built four rental units, with two more planned this year. Assisted husband in building one person siding business to where he is supervising construction crews and contracting to perform the full range of construction and building work, both residential and commercial.

Job 6

03/1985 to 11/1990, 60+ hours per week.

OWNER-OPERATOR, $950,000 gross sales, annually. $60,000 average annual net salary. Sea and Garden Market, Slidell, LA.

Employed up to fifteen personnel. Operated six days per week. Trained staff. Quality control, supplies, inventory, price and cost control, billing, ordering inventory, product, equipment, state and Federal taxes, payroll, W-2s. Completed all required paperwork for necessary state and city, and alcohol licenses. Worked with city and state officials to meet all requirements for restaurant operation.

ACCOMPLISHMENTS: Each year business earned net profits, with steady growth in employees and sales.

EDUCATION

Pearl River High School, Poplarville, MS. 1976, diploma.

NAVOCEANO's Long Term Training Program, completed at William Carey College, Hattiesburg, MS. Business Management, Accounting and Computer Information Systems,

05/2000. GPA: 3.167, 45 semester hours, Dean's List.

Production Management and Policy, Spring 2000; Management Information Policy and Analysis, Spring 2000; Strategic Management and Policy, Spring 2000.

Practicum, Spring 2000; Systems Analysis and Design, Spring 2000; Programming II, Winter 1999; Accounting II, Winter 1999; Public Speaking, Winter 1999.

Economics II, Winter 1999; Database Management Systems, Winter 1999.

Accounting I, Fall 1999; Data Communication and Networks Fall 1999.

Programming I, Fall 1999; Economics I, Fall 1999. General Psychology, Fall 1999.

PROFESSIONAL TRAINING

NAVOCEANO training program.

Intermediate and beginning HTML, 16 hrs, 1999; Intro to ACCESS, 8 hrs, 1999; UNIX, 40 hrs, 1998; Total Quality Leadership, 8 hrs, 1997; Word, 8 hrs, 1996; Word Perfect, 8 hrs, 1995; Oceanography, 8 hrs, 1995; Effective English, 8 hrs, 1995; Navy Correspondence, 8 hrs, 1995; Lotus 1-2-3, 16 hrs, 1995; 21st Century Secretary, 24 hrs, 1995; Communication Skills, 8 hrs, 1995; Harvard Graphics, 24 hrs, 1994; MS DOS, 16 hrs, 1993; Basic Life Seminar, 8 hrs, 1992.

Pearl River Community College, Poplarville, MS. Night classes taken while working full-time. Legal Environment of Business, 1999; Advanced Microcomputer Applications, 1999; Business Communication 1999; College Algebra, 1998; Essentials of Business, 1998; Intermediate Algebra, 1997; Intro Algebra, 1997; Traditional Grammar, 1997; English Comp I & II, 1994, 1996; QuickBooks, 1996.

Coastal College, Slidell, LA, Legal/Medical Secretary, 1992, Associates, Degree, AA, 66 semester hours, GPA: 3.98, High Honors, Dean's List, 1992 and 1991. Top 10% of graduating class.

Delgado College, Slidell, LA.

Beginning Programming and Small Business Management

Professional Licenses and Certificates

Currently studying for Louisiana Builders License.

Performance Ratings, Awards, Honors, and Recognitions

William Carey College Dean's List, 1999.

Notable Achievement Award, NAVOCEANO, 1996, 1999.

Performance Award, Quality Step Increase, NAVOCEANO, 1998.

Coastal College Dean's List, 1991, 1992.

Other Information

COMPUTER PROFICIENCIES—MS Windows, MS Office, MS Word, Access, Word Star, Harvard Graphics, Power Point, DBASE, Fed Forms, Instant Recall, Quicken 3 and 4, Word Perfect, Excel, Lotus, Internet, e-mail, Message Text Format, Basic Programming, UNIX. Create, copy, edit, store, retrieve, print, and standardize documents using a glossary of pre-recorded formats, form letters and mailing lists. Also prepares viewgraphs, maps, charts, spreadsheets, databases, workflow management software, and word-processing documents.

PROBLEM SOLVING AND ANALYTICAL SKILLS—Gather, assemble, organize, and present clear and concise written products. Evaluate customer concerns, determine problems that need to be solved, develop options, and make decision on the most appropriate and efficient course of assuring customer satisfaction. Handle stressful situations with professionalism respect and tact.

PERSONAL STRENGTHS—Competent, professional, proficient, attentive to detail, conscientious and diligent, as noted by supervisor in his recommendation for long-term training. Demonstrated flexibility, adaptability, creativity. Outstanding listening ability; proven oral and written communication skills.

SELF-MOTIVATED—Determines priorities, and plans work assignments independently. Five years experience as small business owner and manager.

CUSTOMER SERVICE—Apply Total Quality, TQ, principles to determine needs of customer and assure complete satisfaction. Listen to feedback to evaluate improvements that may be needed in products or services. Recognize that quality service, and products, and/or customer satisfaction are critical for long term business growth. Train employees to understand and apply TQ in all tasks performed.

Republican Women's Association of St. Tammany Parish.

SUNDAY SCHOOL TEACHER, Grace Memorial Baptist Church, Slidell, LA.

PRESIDENT, Young Women's Sunday School Class,

Women's Small Business Association of St. Tammany Parish.

Habitat for Humanity.

LOCKSMITH, ELECTRONICS WG

MAINTENANCE STRUCTURAL TRADE CHIEF II, CARPENTRY SHOP
CARPENTER
ELECTRONIC TECHNICIAN

JOHN A. GREEN

SSN: 000339999

4450 Country Club Road

Edgewood, MD 21200

Home Phone: 410-555-0111

Work Phone: 410-555-0900

E-mail Address: JAG@netmail.com

EMPLOYMENT HISTORY

Job 1

March 1999-Present, 40 hours per week, **Locksmith, Electronics, Building Security Unit,** $18.00 per hour. University of Maryland, College Park, MD. Physical Plant Department. Supervisor: John Smith, 301 787-8888. May contact.

FIELD INSTALLER, independently or as part of a team. Ensure the security and protection of the University property and individuals through electronic systems. Install, test, maintain and repair electronic security systems throughout the campus. Troubleshoot systems and communicate with contractors concerning warranty and specialized repairs. Oversee contractor performance and assist with logistics of repairs. Install, repair, build, and test mechanical and electronic locks, locking systems, door closures and locks. Survey facilities and make system recommendations.

Communicate with customers concerning problems and develop recommendations and solutions. Provide regular progress reports to university community administrators, faculty and students during installation and troubleshooting of security systems. Participate in security design meetings to support building construction and renovation plans. Responsive to situations, customer problems, and security and safety requirements. Give technical assistance to staff concerning installation of systems, troubleshooting and problem-solving, as well as electronic door and lock troubleshooting, systems installation and repair.

Maintain and update campus security system records of key recipients and key codes. Access computerized systems for updating information in computer databases; updating key codes. Knowledge of electronic access systems, skill in reading and interpreting wiring schematics and architectural drawings, mechanical and mathematics skills, inspection and evaluation of security systems; troubleshooting problems; Occupational Safety and Health Administration, OSHA, Maryland Occupational Safety and Health, MOSH, and Americans with Disabilities Act, ADA requirements concerning security and electronics systems; methods and techniques used in repair, maintenance and installation of locking systems and devices, and door closures.

SPECIAL PROJECTS

—ARCHITECTURAL BUILDING—students were leaving the doors open and non-students were entering and were considered dangerous. Installed an alarm system that deterred students from leaving the doors open effectively eliminating incidences of unwanted visitors.

—McKELDIN LIBRARY—installed the Protag system to more than 200 computers; required installation with panel alarms. Installed the first photo beam system tied to alarm panel.

—ACCESS CONTROL—replaced old system converging from Northern system to Nextel. Level Access control.

—PROGRAMMING—wiring for the MC25 Program involving installation of specialized wring for delayed relays for handicapped door opening systems. Installed more than 200 automatic door openers.

Job 2

07/1988-03/1999, 40 hours per week, **Maintenance Structural Trade Chief II,** $16.75 per hour. Carpentry Shop, University of Maryland Maintenance Shop, 1020 Rhode Island Avenue, College Park, MD 20902. Supervisor: John Jones, 301 111-2222

Coordinated, directed and supervised a crew of six tradesmen performing all the installation and repair of doors, windows, locksets, automatic door closers for campus security. Installed, tested, maintained and repaired electronic security systems and locks throughout the campus. Maintained a five-stage campus-wide master key system. Installed, repaired, rebuilt, tested mechanical and electronic locks, locking systems, door closures and locks. Communicated with university community administrators, faculty and students during installation and troubleshooting of security systems.

Installed systems, performed troubleshooting and resolved problems for electronic locks, doors and overheads. Troubleshoot systems and communicate with contractors concerning warranty and specialized repairs. Participated in security design meetings to support building construction and renovation plans. Maintained and updated records system for the campus security system. Maintenance of records of key recipients and key codes. Prepared departmental reports and updates.

Trained maintenance personnel in troubleshooting and disassembly of locks. Expert in disassembling locks, repair, and replacement of worn tumblers, springs and parts. Demonstrated knowledge of electronic access systems, skill in reading and interpreting wiring schematics and architectural drawings, mechanical and mathematics skills, inspection and evaluating of security systems; troubleshooting problems.

Performed tasks independently initially, or as part of a team for system installation. Ensured the security and protection of the University property and individuals through electronic systems. Responsive to situations, customer problems, and security and safety requirements. Knowledge of OSHA, MOSH and ADA guidelines maintained by the university concerning security and electronics systems. Knowledge of methods and techniques used in repair, maintenance, and installation of locking systems and devices, and door closures.

SPECIAL PROJECTS:

—NORTHERN ACCESS CONTROL replacements and installations.

—LOCK STANDALONE SYSTEMS — V-serial.

—Installed access controls for HANDICAP ACCESS. Resolved an access problem for handicapped operations when a student was unable to open the door after hours.

—Designed and installed a DELAYED RELAY WIRING SYSTEM to enable access to door opening systems after hours.

—CONVERTED KEY LOCK TO CARD LOCK SYSTEM, setting up record-keeping system and updating codes.

—OVERHEAD DOORS — shop expert on overhead door installations and troubleshooting.

Job 3

08/1982-07/1988, **CARPENTER,** $12.50 per hour. University of Maryland, College Park, MD.

Independently planned and executed journeyman level carpentry projects in construction, alteration, repairing, and modifying buildings and structures, fittings, panels, partitions, and other wood or wood substitute components. Carried out associated work such as painting, sheet metal, plumbing, and electrical. Applied technical knowledge when utilizing drawings, sketches, blueprints. Interpreted and applied specifications, making adjustments as necessary. Selected and ordered lumber, materials, and supplies to assure quality and durability relative to intended use.

Installed rafters, studs, sills, plate braces, joists, floors, sub-floors, panels, siding sheeting, roofing, building paper, insulating materials, door and window frames, and interior and exterior trim. Repaired or replaced floors, wall or coiling tile, including dropped ceilings. Performed glazing, lockset installation, roof repairs, screening, countertops, cabinets, and paneling; plumbing and electrical incidental to carpentry work including moving fixtures, fittings, pumps, outlets, etc. when moving or installing sheetrock. Maintained appropriate inventory of tools and equipment, identified any special needs, and prepared order for project specifications.

Job 4

1980 — 1982, U.S. Army, **CARPENTER,** Honorably Discharged.

EDUCATION

Annapolis Senior High School, Annapolis, MD. 1979, diploma.

University of Maryland, College Park, MD. 1986, 25 semester hours.

SPECIALIZED TRAINING

National Training School, the National Burglar and Fire Alarm Association, NBFAA, Central Station Alarm Association and the Security Industry Association, 1999.

National Training School, Eldridge MD, Certified Access Control Technician. Completed a one-year training program which includes seminars conducted by the NBFAA convention, NBFAA chapter association seminars, classes conducted by security industry association members; seminars at the International Security Conferences; classes conducted by manufacturers or distributors; and educational training provided to the alarm industry, 1999.

Anne Arundel County College, Annapolis, MD.

Fundamental Woodworking, 3 semester hours, 1998.

Machine Woodworking, 3 semester hours, 1998.

Woodworking Technician, 3 semester hours, 1997.

Technical Calculations, 3 semester hours, 1997.

Mechanical Drawing I, 3 semester hours, 1997.

Maryland Fire and Rescue Institute, Trench Construction and Safety, 16 hours, 1990.

Maryland State Department of Training, Leadership Challenges of the '90s, 24 hours, 1990.

Maryland State Department of Training, Communication Styles and Strategies, 24 hours, 1990.

Community Associations Institute, Leadership Training Program, 16 hours, 1989.

Maryland State Department of Training, Principles of Supervision, 40 hours, 1988.

LICENSES and CERTIFICATES

Certified Alarm Technician, 1999.

Certified Access Control Technician, 1999.

System 9760 Installation Certification, 1999.

Certified Forklift Operator, University of Maryland at College Park, Physical Plant, 1999.

AWARDS

Letter of Commendation—"provided an innovative hanging system which allowed us to mount a very heavy plaque onto a brick wall. The project presented a number of problems, all of which were resolved skillfully by Mr. John A. Green." Donald King, Chancellor, 1992.

OTHER INFORMATION

Active volunteer with the Humane Society. Assist with fundraising and publicity programs to promote good homes for animals. Volunteer approximately 10 hours per week.

Co-workers and supervisors recognize my attention to detail, quality workmanship and dependability in meeting project deadlines. Always strive to meet customer expectations and respond to their needs.

SUMMARY OF SKILLS

ELECTRONIC TECHNICIAN—installation, testing, troubleshooting, repairing, and maintaining, electronic security systems. Electronic locks, door closures, alarms. Security systems design, record systems of key codes and key recipients.

MAINTENANCE MECHANIC—automatic and mechanical locks. Disassembly, repair, replacement of parts. Systems evaluation, design, and consultation with university administrators. Knowledge of applicable OSHA, MOSH, and ADA guidelines for locking systems and devices, and door closures.

CONSTRUCTION AND CARPENTRY—carpentry and incidental work including construction, installation, alteration, repair, painting, glazing, sheet metal, plumbing, electrical. Project planning utilizing blueprints. Selection of materials and supplies. Maintaining tool and equipment inventory.

SUPERVISOR AND TEAM LEADER—coordination, direction, supervision of six mechanics and carpenters for all campus security needs. Training in techniques and methods of troubleshooting, repair, maintenance, installation of security systems and devices. Team leadership in assuring project completion in accordance with established timetable, quality, and performance standards.

COMMUNICATION AND CUSTOMER SERVICES—determination of customer needs through security design meetings. Progress reports to university administrators concerning systems diagnosis and options for problem solving and remediation. Liaison with contractors overseeing performance, and coordinating warranty and specialized repairs.

Appendix B:
Department of Defense Employment Web Sites

VACANCY ANNOUNCEMENTS AND ON-LINE APPLICATION WEB SITES

ARMY CIVILIAN JOBS — Click on Employment
http://cpol.army.mil/

AIR FORCE CIVILIAN JOBS
http://www.afpc.randolph.af.mil/resWeb
https://www.afpc.randolph.af.mil/resWeb/resume/resume.htm

Civilian Announcement Notification System
https://www.afpc.randolph.af.mil/resWeb/cans.htm

U.S. NAVY and U.S. MARINE CORPS CIVILIAN JOBS —
Click on Jobs, Jobs Jobs
www.donhr.navy.mil

WASHINGTON HEADQUARTERS SERVICE (WHS)
http://persec.whs.mil/hrsc/empinfo.html

Civilian Job Kit:
http://persec.whs.mil/hrsc/instruct.html

DEFENSE FINANCE AND ACCOUNTING SERVICES — Kansas City
http://www.dfas.mil/people/kcdeu/

DEFENSE FINANCE AND ACCOUNTING SERVICES — Regional Service Center
http://www.dfas.mil/jobs/

DEFENSE LOGISTICS AGENCY (DLA)
http://www.hroc.dla.mil/jobcntrl.htm

OFFICE OF PERSONNEL MANAGEMENT

VACANCY ANNOUNCEMENTS AND RESUME BUILDER

OPM Job Vacancy Announcements and the Resume Builder
www.usajobs.opm.gov

NON-DOD WEB SITES FOR ON-LINE APPLICATIONS AND VACANCY ANNOUNCEMENTS

DEPARTMENT OF ENERGY
https://jobsonline.doe.gov/

NATIONAL IMAGERY AND MAPPING AGENCY (NIMA)
http://www.nima.mil/

U.S. GEOLOGICAL SURVEY JOBS
http://www.usgs.gov/ohr/

CENTRAL INTELLIGENCE AGENCY (CIA)
http://www.odci.gov/cia/employment/resume.html

 Tip These web site addresses may change. Please bookmark the correct sites.

GLOSSARY

ACRONYMS — See individual acronyms.

CAREER DECISIONS — Since the new system requires one resume and many applicants have interests in more than one job series, applicants have to make career decisions before writing and submitting their resume. They can add another job series by updating their resume or submitting the "self-nomination form."

CONTEXT — Those portions of the narrative content of a job application which describe the occupationally distinguishing characteristics of processes being used, tasks being performed or systems with which an applicant is familiar or in which he or she possesses on-the-job experience.

CONTINUOUSLY OPEN — Vacancy Announcements written for automated human resources recruitments are "open continuously" so that applicants can submit their resume anytime to an applicant "inventory." HR recruiters subsequently search these inventories to build referral lists of the best-qualified candidates when hiring managers request a new hire.

CPAC — Civilian Personnel Advisory Council

CPOC — Civilian Personnel Office Center

CREDITING PLANS — Some hiring managers in some agencies will still write crediting plans. But most hiring managers will simply be writing position descriptions for the new positions. The crediting plan is a plan with points assigned to each knowledge, skill and ability. Crediting plans are used by ranking panels to rank all qualified candidates and determine which candidates are in the final "Best Qualified" group.

DATABASE SEARCH — The human resources recruiter will search for qualified applicants by matching the knowledge, skills, and abilities in the position description with resumes in the Resumix database.

DESIGNATED EXAMINING UNIT (DEU) — An office established by a Federal agency under specific authority granted by the Office of Personnel Management for the purpose of recruiting outside job candidates. DEUs not only determine basic candidate qualifications, but rate and rank job candidates and establish registers of candidates for referral to selecting officials. Once an outside candidate is rated and ranked and placed on a register of qualified candidates, he or she is referred to as "eligible" for competitive appointment in the particular government agency serviced by the DEU.

ELECTRONIC DATABASE — A collection of data from electronic Resumes that have been scanned and stored for referral against future job vacancies. The modern equivalent of an application inventory.

ELIGIBILITY — The status of being "hirable" by a Federal agency based on an applicant's personal candidate "status." For example, former Federal employees who were continuously employed on non-temporary positions for three consecutive years may be eligible to be hired by Federal agencies due to their status as "re-instatement eligible." Other Federal job seekers must gain eligibility for initial appointment by some other means, i.e., applying under an agency job announcement or being placed on a roster of candidates as announced by a "Designated Examining Unit."

GENERAL GRAMMAR — The Resumix and other automated software includes artificial intelligence that includes a large vocabulary of words and skills (40,000 of them). The words are general words that describe jobs in general. They are not specific to government; they describe jobs. The general grammar is the database of phrases upon which a resume will be matched. There is not list of the general grammar available to the general public.

GENERIC VACANCY ANNOUNCEMENT or INVENTORY BUILDING ANNOUNCEMENT — Vacancy announcements for Federal jobs have changed to become generic. They are shorter and cover general knowledge, skills and abilities for any job in a series. Previous styles of writing vacancy announcements included details of the specific job. The new announcements are shorter and broader. They are called inventory-building announcements because the announcements are generally opened in order to "build an inventory of applicants."

HR — Human Resources

HROC — Human Resources Office Center

JOB KIT — A document usually associated with automated, electronic staffing processes (i.e., Resumix) which normally provide candidates with formatting and data element explanations and instructions to be used in preparing an acceptable application for submission in order to receive consideration for vacant positions.

KNOWLEDGE, SKILLS, AND ABILITIES (KSAs) — Certain knowledge, skills, and abilities are required to perform a certain job. The format for writing KSAs is different with the new automated HR systems. The former application method in government required an application form and separate KSAs written on pieces of paper. Now the KSAs should still be included, but within the work experience section in the resume.

KNOWLEDGE BASE OF RESUME — 40,000 phrases which are single words, phrases, acronyms, company names, degrees, titles, and so forth.

LOCAL GRAMMAR — Federal human resources offices are building the local grammar of their particular agencies. However, the emphasis on the searches for applicants is not dependent upon the local grammar. The general grammar is 90% of the search. The HR offices are continuing to build the agency's local grammar based on position descriptions, agency missions, programs, and products.

MERIT PROMOTION — A process in Federal government whereby qualified candidates are competitively ranked and considered for promotions based upon their eligibility, their qualifications and their overall knowledge, skills, and abilities.

MINIMUM QUALIFICATIONS — The quality and length of general experience, specialized experience and/or education an applicant must possess in order to qualify for consideration for possible entry into a specific occupation, position and grade. Candidate applications must demonstrate possession of minimum qualifications before they can be further considered in the second major phase of the staffing process, rating and ranking. (The word "eligible" in Federal Personnel parlance simply implies a person is "hirable"...but does not speak to the person's qualifications for the position.)

ONE RESUME FITS ALL — The automated human resource systems all require that the applicant write one resume for multiple job interests. The new ONE RESUME concept means that the applicant has to think about specific job interests and focus the resume at one time toward as many as 2 to 4 serious job interests. This is a viable process with the ability to use 2 to 5 pages of copy, depending on the HR Job Kit Instructions.

ONE-STEP HR PROCESS — Some agencies use a one-step process for submitting resumes. The applicant sends in their resume and completes the additional data sheet (which is in the Resume Builder) and simply waits for e-mails from HR saying they are found qualified. There is no need to search for vacancy announcements or prepare a self-nomination.

PERFORMANCE PAY PLAN OR DEMONSTRATION PAY PLANS — A performance pay plan is a special "merit pay" plan developed with the intent of rewarding employees for their level of actual job performance. The General Manager ("GM") pay experiment for Federal sector supervisors and managers (no longer in effect) was an example of a performance pay plan. Demonstration pay plans are special "temporary" incentive pay plans authorized by The Office of Personnel Management (OPM) as part of formally approved Demonstration Projects ("Demos"). Demos are conducted under the auspices of OPM, or under its supervision, to determine whether a specified change in personnel management policies or procedures would result in improved Federal personnel management and compensation methods, resulting in a more motivated and productive Federal workforce. Demonstration pay plans, like other performance pay plans, provide pay incentives for employees who are excellent and superior performers, rather than uniform pay increases to all employees based upon longevity and fully satisfactory job performance.

RATING AND RANKING — The process of measuring the overall relevance of an applicant's total background to the specific skill, knowledge, and ability criteria of a position being filled. This normally involves the assignment of "point values" for a range of career attributes that may include experience, education, training, performance appraisal rating, and awards. Rated applications are compared with the minimum point values and other requirements governing referral eligibility. Those meeting cutoff criteria are placed in alphabetical order on a certificate of referral for consideration by the selecting official. Resumix and other automated software packages will rate and rank the applicants when the HR professional searches under certain knowledge, skills, and abilities. The software will rate and rank the candidates by number. Those applicants with the highest number under the search will be rated the highest. Those rated the highest will be reviewed for minimum qualifications and be forwarded to the hiring manager.

RESUME BUILDER — The Resume Builder is an on-line form for writing or copying and pasting your resume so that the resume can be entered into the Resumix database. The Resume Builder is not part of Resumix system, but simply a way to enter the data, update, and submit the resume. Each agency has its own Resume Builder as part of their Job Kits. Job Kit and Resume Builder addresses are located at our Weblink Page.

RESUMIX — Resumix™ a HotJobs.com, LTD company, Sunnyvale, CA, is an off-the-shelf staffing systems technology that matches jobs and applicants. The Department of Defense has mandated that many DOD agencies use Resumix systems to improve the efficiency and quality of matching applicant skills with personnel needs. The Resumix recruitment system requires applicants to write a simple 2- to 5-page resume for Federal applications. Resumix is a computerized software program which is knowledge-based and which uses artificial intelligence to read and analyze job applications in context. Resumix rates applications and produces a ranked list of candidates. It does not review applications for the possession of minimum qualifications. This function is performed by personnel specialists.

RESUMIX RESUME — An electronic resume written for the Resumix system. The Resumix resume is a good resume that includes the knowledge, skills and abilities, education, employment, work descriptions, accomplishments and other information that describes a person's career. The information should be relevant to the career interests of the applicant. The format of the Resumix resume is plain looking with no bold, italics, bullets, shadows, or indents. The computer software has to "read" the resume content.

SELECTING SUPERVISOR, SELECTING OFFICIAL, HIRING MANAGER — The hiring manager will receive up to 15 of the highest ranked candidates based on the Resumix search and the quick review by the HR person for minimum qualifications. The Hiring Manager will then read the paper resumes, perform telephone or in-person interviews and make selections. The Personnel Office generally follows up by making actual job offers.

SELF-NOMINATION — (two uses) The Air Force, Army, Navy and other DOD agencies use a self-nomination form for applicants to "self-nominate them-selves" for vacancy announcements that they find on their Web sites. Applicants have already prepared their resumes and submitted them to the database. When the applicants find an announcement, they will complete the self-nomination form and submit online, by e-mail or fax. If they do not self-nominate, they will not be considered for positions. This differs from previously used referral systems, for example in the former Air Force system where civilians "pre-registered" against all vacancies for which they qualified in specified geographic locations, were automatically referred and notified after their name was referred to a selecting official.
The Navy and Marines use a "self-nomination" which is called APPLICATION EXPRESS for nominating for jobs.

SKILLS BUCKET — That portion of an applicant's Resumix *resume summary* database which retains (stores) all of the valid skills, knowledge, and abilities (KSAs) contained in an application as identified by the electronic Resumix software review and analysis. Resumix skills buckets have a finite capacity in terms of the number of valid KSAs that can be retained within them. This highlights the need for relevance and brevity in developing narrative application content.

VETERANS EMPLOYMENT OPPORTUNITIES ACT (VEOA) — Veterans Employment Opportunities Act (VEOA). Allows preference eligibles or veterans who are honorably discharged from the armed forces after 3 or more years of active service to compete for vacant positions, if the hiring agency is accepting applications from individuals outside its own workforce under merit promotion procedures.

VETERAN'S READJUSTMENT APPOINTMENT (VRA) — The VRA is a special authority by which agencies can, if they wish, appoint an eligible veteran without competition.

Standard Automated Inventory and Referral System (STAIRS)

STAIRS is an automated inventory and referral system which uses a commercial off the shelf software product called *Resumix*, and other information systems technology such as scanning, optical character recognition, artificial intelligence, interactive voice response (IVR), and the Internet. It eliminates most paper and many manual processes involved in the acceptance and referral of internal and external candidates for positions. STAIRS was developed to operate in a regional environment where all processing and referral is done at a central location. STAIRS is the human resources system being used by the Department of Defense agencies.

STAIRS has three major processes:

1. **Announcement process.** Used to solicit applications from individuals not already in the database inventory.

2. **Application process.** This process differs for external and internal candidates. In both cases, however, applicants use a *resume* to describe their experience, education and training.

3. **Fill process.** In this process, a job analysis is conducted using major job requirements and knowledge, skills and abilities (KSAs) from the position description and additional information provided by the manager. A search plan is developed using required and desirable criteria, and these criteria are automatically compared against the extracted information in the Resumix database to identify the highly qualified candidates for referral.

TWO-STEP REVIEW PROCESS — Most agencies use a two-step process for applying for jobs. First applicants submit a resume. Second, they search for vacancy announcements that are relevant and complete a self-nomination form for consideration of positions. If an applicant does not search for announcements and submit the self-nomination, he or she will not be considered for the job.

VACANCY AND FLYER NUMBER, ANNOUNCEMENT NUMBER — The number that is found on the top of the vacancy announcement which identifies the announcement.

VACANCY ANNOUNCEMENTS — The listings of open jobs in government. The announcements include the name of the hiring agency, location (some-times), title of position, grade levels available, and a general description of the job. The announcement also includes details regarding veteran's preferences, services for disabled persons, and other personnel information. The announcement will give some instructions on how to apply for jobs through their particular human resources office. The Navy and Marines vacancy announcements include links to the Resume Builder. Scroll to the bottom of the vacancy announcement and open the Resume Builder.

WORK EXPERIENCE OUTLINE — A clear outline of the activities an employee actually carries out in the course of their job, and the roles a person plays, resulting in an organized and logical description of experienced gained on a given job. The work experience outline is used in writing a work description that becomes part of a resume.

WORK HISTORY — The sum total of a person's employment background, including paid positions, volunteer work and any other work (such as self-employment) through which a person obtains qualifying experience.

Major Concepts and Terms OPM Qualification Manual

Major concepts and terms, defined in the Office of Personnel Management's Qualifications Manual, follow below in alphabetical order.

Accredited Education is education above the high school level completed in a U.S. college, university, or other educational institution that has been accredited by one of the accrediting agencies or associations recognized by the Secretary, U.S. Department of Education.

Competitive Appointment is an appointment to a position in the competitive service following open competitive examination or under direct-hire authority. The competitive examination, which is open to all applicants, may consist of a written test, an evaluation of an applicant's education and experience, and/or an evaluation of other attributes necessary for successful performance in the position to be filled.

Competitive Service includes all positions in which appointments are subject to the provisions of Chapter 33 of title 5, United States Code. Positions in the executive branch of the Federal Government are in the competitive service unless they are specifically excluded from it. Positions in the legislative and judicial branches are outside of the competitive service unless they are specifically included in it.

Concurrent Experience is experience gained in more than one position, during the same period of time, with either the same employer or with a different employer.

Education Above the High School Level (or Post High-School Education) is successfully completed progressive study at an accredited business or technical school, junior college, college, or university where the institution normally requires a high school diploma or equivalent for admission.

Fill-in Employment is employment held by persons during the time period after leaving their regular occupation in anticipation of, but before entering, military service.

Foreign Education is education acquired outside of any State of the U.S., the District of Columbia, the Commonwealth of Puerto Rico, a Trust Territory of the Pacific Islands, or any territory or possession of the U.S.

Graduate Education is successfully completed education in a graduate program for which a bachelor's or higher degree is normally required for admission. To be creditable, such education must show evidence of progress through a set curriculum, i.e., it is part of a program leading to a master's or higher degree, and not education consisting of undergraduate and/or continuing education courses that do not lead to an advanced degree.

Group Coverage (or Generic) Qualification Standards are standards prescribed for groups of occupational series that have a common pattern of education, experience, and/or other requirements.

High School Graduation or Equivalent means the applicant has received a high school diploma, General Education Development (GED) equivalency certificate, or proficiency certificate from a State or territorial-level Board or Department of Education.

Individual Occupational Requirements are requirements e.g., experience or education, for particular occupational series or positions within a series and are used in conjunction with a group coverage (generic) standard.

Inservice Placement includes a noncompetitive action in which a position is filled with a current or former competitive service employee through promotion, reassignment, change to lower grade, transfer, reinstatement, reemployment, or restoration. Inservice placement also includes noncompetitive conversion of appointees whose Federal excepted positions are brought into the competitive service under title 5 CFR 316.702, and Department of Defense/Nonappropriated Fund (DOD/NAF) and Coast Guard NAF employees whose positions are brought into the competitive service.

Knowledge, Skills, and Abilities (KSA's) are the attributes required to perform a job and are generally demonstrated through qualifying experience, education, or training. Knowledge is a body of information applied directly to the performance of a function. Skill is an observable competence to perform a learned psychomotor act. Ability is competence to perform an observable behavior or a behavior that results in an observable product.

Modification of an OPM qualification standard for inservice placement actions means agency or OPM substitution of qualification requirements different from those in the published standard. While applicants who qualify under a modified standard do not meet all of the specific requirements described in the published standard, their overall background show evidence of their potential success in the position to be filled. A modified standard may apply to any number of positions in an organization.

Noncompetitive Action means an appointment to or placement in a position in the competitive service that is not made by selection from an open competitive examination, and that is usually based on current or prior Federal service. A noncompetitive action includes (1) all of the types of actions described under inservice placement, above; (2) appointments of non-Federal employees whose public or private enterprise positions are brought into the competitive service under title 5 CFR 316.701; and (3) appointments and conversions to career and career-conditional employment made under special authorities covered in 5 CFR 315, Subpart F.

Normal Line of Promotion (or Progression) is the pattern of upward movement from one grade to another for a position or group of positions in an organization.

Outside the Register Appointment means an appointment in the competitive service made under an agency's applicant supply system because either there is not a sufficient number of eligibles on the appropriate register or no competitor inventory exists. Agencies are also authorized to make temporary limited appointments outside the register at grades GS-12 and below.

Position means the officially assigned duties and responsibilities that make up the work performed by an employee.

Quality Ranking Factors are knowledge, skills, and abilities that could be expected to enhance significantly performance in a position, but are not essential for satisfactory performance. Applicants who possess such KSA's may be ranked above those who do not, but no one may be rated ineligible solely for failure to possess such KSA's.

Related Education is education above the high school level that has equipped the applicant with the knowledge, skills, and abilities to perform successfully the duties of the position being filled. Education may relate to the duties of a specific position or to the occupation, but must be appropriate for the position being filled.

Research Positions are positions in professional series that primarily involve scientific inquiry or investigation, or research-type exploratory development of a creative or scientific nature, where the knowledge required to perform the work successfully is acquired typically and primarily through graduate study. The positions are such that the academic preparation will equip the applicant to perform fully the work after a short orientation period.

Selective Factors are knowledge, skills, abilities, or special qualifications that are in addition to the minimum requirements in a qualification standard, but are determined to be essential to perform the duties and responsibilities of a particular position. Applicants who do not meet a selective factor are ineligible for further consideration.

Series or Occupational Series means positions similar as to specialized work and qualification requirements. Series are designated by a title and number such as the Accounting Series, GS-510; the Secretary Series, GS-318; and the Microbiology Series, GS-403.

Specialized Experience is experience that has equipped the applicant with the particular knowledge, skills, and abilities to perform successfully the duties of the position and is typically in or related to the work of the position to be filled.

Waiver of an OPM qualification standard involves setting aside requirements in a published standard to place an employee in a particular position, usually to avoid some kind of hardship to the employee, such as in cases of reduction in force or administrative error on the part of the agency. Extra training and/or skills development may be needed to help the employee adjust to the new position. Waivers are granted by OPM or an agency, as appropriate, on a case-by-case basis, and do not directly affect other positions in the organization.

Work-Study Programs are government or non-government programs that provide supervised work experience related to a student's course of study and are a part of, or a supplement to, education. Federal student-trainee programs are examples of such programs.

About the Authors

Contributing Authors

BRIAN FRIEL, Chapter 1, Commercial Activities

Brian Friel is an associate editor for Government Executive magazine. He previously ran the news operation at Planetgov.com and was managing editor for GovExec.com. He has written more than 1,500 articles about government management, technology, procurement, careers, pay and benefits, and other public administration topics. He has interviewed the leaders of many Federal agencies. Brian serves as the editor for Career Corner, the weekly career advice column that appears at resume-place.com every Tuesday.

CHRISTOPHER JUGE, Chapter 11, Plain Language

Award-winning author, lecturer, and trial attorney Christopher Juge has nearly twenty years' professional writing experience in the corporate, legal, and government spheres. His writing and oral skills have been battle-tested and proven effective: in twelve years of litigation in New York City, Mr. Juge has won more than 99% of his court battles, including hundreds of Federal and State motions and trials, class actions, and major media cases involving up to one billion dollars. He is currently a senior executive in the largest foster care agency in the world.

Educated at the Sorbonne and the Ecole Nationale des Sciences Politiques, in Paris, France, Mr. Juge is also a French/English interpreter, a professional portrait artist (his official portrait of the former Chief Judge of the State of New York hangs in the Sullivan County Museum in New York), the soloist in his church, and a student of the martial arts.

MARK C. REICHENBACHER, Resumix Resume Samples, CD-ROM

Mark Reichenbacher has a distinguished career of over twenty-three years in Federal sector labor management relations. He has acquired a well-rounded portfolio of experience, having held generalist, specialist, supervisory, and managerial positions at the field and headquarters levels. Currently, he serves as Branch Chief for a nationwide labor management relations program.

His career is distinguished by his reputation as a coach and mentor. In his agency, he has taken initiative and voluntarily developed training materials in how to complete applications for promotion, along with delivering seminars to employees on how best to present their qualifications and experience to give them the strongest competitive position possible. He also is contributing editor for publications written by Ms. Troutman. For the past five years, he has been a professional resume writer for Federal and private sector clients having a variety of occupational backgrounds and career interests.

Mark holds a Masters of Science degree in Labor Studies degree and a Bachelors of Arts degree in Psychology and Economics. Currently his family resides in Manassas, Virginia.

Kathryn Kraemer Troutman

Kathryn Kraemer Troutman is recognized worldwide as the pioneer designer of the Federal Resume, which she created in 1995 with her first book, *The Federal Resume Guidebook & PC Disk*. Ms. Troutman is a respected author, a highly acclaimed columnist on www.govexec.com (with the popular Career Corner now at www.resume-place.com), and an inspirational workshop leader of the Federal government and Department of Defense. She was the inspiring host for a 75-minute video introducing the National Security Agency Internal Staffing Resume for more than 4,000 NSA employees. She was a speaker on "Best Practices in Recruitment" for the International Personnel Manager's Association in Hershey, PA, introducing the Department of Defense's automated systems to public service human resources managers, Summer, 2000. She is an experienced career trainer in Federal government and Department of Defense agencies.

As a founding board member of the National Association of Women Business Owners, Ms. Troutman is a veteran business entrepreneur. Her upcoming books include the Federal Senior Executive Service Candidate's Guidebook and the Non-DOD version of the Electronic Federal Resume Guidebook.

When Ms. Troutman founded The Resume Place, Inc. in 1971, she established locations in Washington D.C. and Baltimore. Since its birth, The Resume Place has been and is the leading resume consulting and training firm on the Internet. www.resume-place.com, a pioneering Web site established in 1995, is the place where more than 12,000 visitors find information on resume writing for Federal and private industry every month. It is the preferred provider of resume writing training, professional writing services, and all other career development services for the U.S. Federal Government.

The Resume Place, Inc. - Professional Writing Services

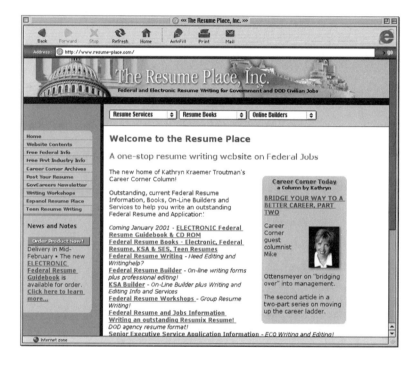

http://www.resume-place.com

Professional Writing, Design and Editing Services for: Electronic Resumes, Private Industry Resumes, One-page Networking Resume, Federal Resumes, KSAs, and Senior Executive Service applications; Interviewing Training and Role-playing.

Full-Service Writing and Editing

Need help with writing an outstanding, professional resume that presents the best experience and skills you have to offer? Want a free estimate for professional services? Send your past applications, resume, position descriptions and any vacancy announcements that can be helpful in finding keywords. Expert electronic resume writers can draft your Resumix or Federal resume based on the specific Job Kit instructions. We'll research the keywords for up to two occupations for inclusion in your resume. A free estimate with checklist of services will be sent to you by return mail or e-mail.

Send information to: Resume Place, 89 Mellor Ave., Baltimore, MD 21228

Questions? Call (888) 480-8265.

Fax: (410) 744-0112 — Fax up to 10 pages anytime for free estimate.

E-mail attached files to resume@resume-place.com.

Resumix Critique Service

Send the draft of your electronic resume to resume@resume-place.com for a professional critique. The critique and edit will cover content, style of writing, strength of keywords for up to two occupational series, use of accomplishments and use of the active voice. You will receive an edited resume with detailed individual comments within five working days for a fee of $200.00. E-mail your best draft to: resume@resume-place.com.

DOD Agency Job Search Consulting

Need answers to specific questions? Problem announcements and application processes? Job Search consultation and strategies are provided by expert, knowledgeable Federal job search consultants for $100 per hour. We can help you understand the new application processes — application by application.

Resume Writing and Job Search Training

Kathryn Troutman and her team of resume experts can provide resume writing and job search training throughout the U.S to Federal and Department of Defense agencies. Writing an excellent resume, packaging an entire government career, and building the confidence to present accomplishment is challenging for everyone! Kathryn is informative, inspiring, and educates individuals on how to write outstanding resumes. Specific resume samples can be presented to meet the various agency's format requirements. Training covers content development, focus on accomplishments and skills, writing and editing skills, and conversion from employment forms to a resume format. Contact Kathryn at resume@resume-place.com

The Resume Place Press - Publication List

FEDERAL RESUME BOOKS:

Order online, secure order form/shopping cart:

http://www.resume-place.com

Multiple copies: Please call for discounts

> The Resume Place, Inc.
> Small, woman-owned business, ISBN 52-1905077
> Toll-free: (888) 480-8265
> Fax: (410) 744-0112
> 89 Mellor Road
> Baltimore, MD 21228

The ELECTRONIC Federal Resume Guidebook & CD-ROM, 2001, 250 pp., softcover, ISBN: 0-9647025-2-5, $44.95

> The first and only book on how to write the Resumix resume required by the STAIRS system in all Department of Defense agencies.
>
> Chapter 3 "Job Kits Made Easier" interprets the instructions for Army, Navy, Marines, Air Force, and other DOD agencies. Learn about Resume Builders, keywords, and skills summaries.
>
> The CD-ROM includes keywords for 124 Federal jobs and "skills bucket" summaries. The CD-ROM is designed as a Web site and is usable for both PC and Macintosh. Eighteen sample electronic resumes are included in Microsoft Word so that resume writers can use the resumes as a "word template."
>
> This book is a must if you want to apply for a job with a DOD agency, or if you want to get promoted or change civilian jobs.

The Federal Resume Guidebook & PC Disk, 2nd Edition, 1999, 416 pp., softcover, ISBN: 1-56370-545-1, $36.95

> Over 25,000 copies sold nationwide.
>
> The best source available for Federal career transition centers as the style guide for writing a competitive Federal resume.
>
> Features excellent samples of Federal resumes and step-by-step instructions for writing them.

Twenty excellent Federal resume samples and a great chapter on writing KSAs!

Includes comprehensive chapters on KSA's, SES Executive Core Qualifications.

Valuable chapter on editing and converting the lengthy SF-171 descriptions into short, concise, accomplishment-based work experience descriptions.

Creating Your High School Resume, 1998, 144 pp., 8.5 x 11, softcover, 1-56370-508-7, $12.95

A great new workbook that shows how to turn high school classes, activities, and accomplishments into teen resumes that get results!

Creating Your High School Resume gives students the edge when applying for jobs, scholarships, and internships. Whether college-bound or going straight to work, resumes help students articulate and document their skills, natural abilities, interests, and experiences.

Students Learn to Articulate Their Assets. An important aspect of creating resumes is that students learn to articulate what they have to offer. Resumes are a great way to document school clubs and activities, volunteer work, and completed internships — to name just a few!

Resource and Exercise Sheets. Students answer straightforward questions to quickly define their skills and interests. Then they build their own resumes section by section!

Case Studies from Real Students! Many case studies, plus lots of examples show students first hand how to focus, organize, write, and format resumes.

2002 Resume Place Publications

Reinvention Federal Resumes, 2nd Edition

The Senior Executive Service Candidate's Guidebook

ELECTRONIC Federal Resume Guidebook & CD-ROM — Non-DOD version

Other Resume Writing Products

Resumix Resume Writing Builder

http://www.resume-place.com/fedres_builder/index.html

Write your resume with the help of on-line forms, instructions and samples.

KSA Writing Builder

http://www.resume-place.com/ksa_builder/index.html

KSA Writing with Context-Challenge-Action-Results fields, instructions and samples.

Federal Career Corner Archives

http://www.federalcareers.net/

Two years of columns written by Kathryn Kraemer Troutman. Inspiring, Motivating and Instructional in Federal Career Development.

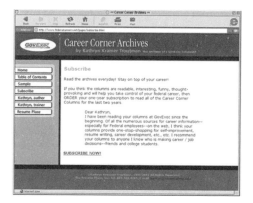

RESUMIX RESUME WRITING WORKSHOP PARTICIPANT REVIEWS

Rational for providing training in Pensacola, Great Lakes, Corpus Christi, San Diego and Norfolk: "Due to Regionalization, Commercial Activities, and government restructuring efforts, personnel in our command have been requesting training on how to write an effective SF171, OF612, or resume. With the implementation of the new Resume Builder program, we took this opportunity to provide this needed service to our employees in learning skills on how to write an effective resume. The training branch requested funds from the command to pay for this effort to make our employees more competitive in the current environment. Senior officials in the command recognized the short and long term benefits of this effort which will aid in the identification of qualified candidates through the HRO Resume Builder/Job Announcement process."

Victoria Knight. NETPDTC

PARTICIPANT REVIEWS:

"I don't know how you found about Kathy, but she is an outstanding instructor. The class was super. I had been my putting this project off for the longest, but now I am almost finished. Before attended this class, I was really lost and did not know where to start. Now the shot is not so painful :-). I truly hope everyone will attend this class."

"The training was very informative, and the Instructor was well versed in the subject and easy to understand. After attending, I realize that I would have been lost trying to do it on my own."

"I don't usually send these kind of e-mails regarding training but I wanted to let you know the Resumix Class was excellent and well worth the time and money the command has spent on this training. The teacher knows her subject and is very good at getting the info across. I think NETPDTC employees are fortunate to have had this opportunity!"

"Thank you for bringing Kathryn Troutman to teach the resume writing class. I have been in the government over 25 years now and it was one of the best government sponsored classes that I have ever been to. Resumes are not one of people's favorite subjects, and I wasn't exactly looking forward to

the class with great expectations. I was very pleasantly surprised to find out that Kathryn made the class live for me. She pointed out things I was doing wrong, and showed me how to do them correctly. She is indeed a subject matter expert and an accomplished communicator/motivator."

"Thank you for the training and in particular for the instructor, Kathryn Troutman! She is outstanding! Positive, knowledgeable, interesting, helpful and keeps you interest up. Thanks for the book too."

"Thanks so much for providing such a worthwhile and valuable trainer. I just wanted to let you know that I thoroughly enjoyed the resume writing course yesterday. Kathryn has very informative and helpful.

I felt that I got so much good, useful information from her. My resumes will be much better now. This was certainly one of the best classes that I have attended in some time."